# The Wiersbe
## BIBLE STUDY SERIES

# The
# Wiersbe
# BIBLE STUDY SERIES

Following the

King of Kings

MATTHEW

transforming lives together

THE WIERSBE BIBLE STUDY SERIES: MATTHEW
Published by David C Cook
4050 Lee Vance Drive
Colorado Springs, CO 80918 U.S.A.

Integrity Music Limited, a Division of David C Cook
Eastbourne, East Sussex BN23 6NT, England

The graphic circle C logo is a registered trademark of David C Cook.

All Scripture quotations in this study are taken from the *Holy Bible, New
International Version®. NIV®.* Copyright © 1973, 1978, 1984 by International
Bible Society. Used by permission of Zondervan. All rights reserved.

In *Be Loyal* excerpts, all Scripture quotations, unless otherwise noted, are
taken from the King James Version of the Bible. (Public Domain.) Scripture
quotations marked NASB are taken from the *New American Standard Bible*, ©
Copyright 1960, 1995 by The Lockman Foundation. Used by permission.

All excerpts taken from *Be Loyal,* second edition, published by
David C Cook in 2008 © 1980 Warren W. Wiersbe, ISBN 978-1-4347-6779-0

ISBN 978-1-4347-6512-3
eISBN 978-0-7814-0376-4

The Team: Steve Parolini, Karen Lee-Thorp, Amy Kiechlin,
Sarah Schultz, Jack Campbell, and Karen Athen
Series Cover Design: John Hamilton Design
Cover Photo: Veer Inc.

Printed in the United States of America
First Edition 2010

8 9 10 11 12 13 14 15 16 17

103118

# Contents

# Introduction to Matthew

## A Most Important Book

Many Bible scholars have called "The Gospel According to Matthew" the most important single document of the Christian faith. Historians tell us that this book was the most widely read, and the most quoted, in the early church.

This Bible study is an overview of Matthew's gospel and focuses on key stories and teachings. For more depth, read the book *Be Loyal*, which, while also not comprehensive, offers a great deal more detail on this most important of Gospels.

## Three Purposes

Twenty or thirty years after Jesus had gone back to heaven, a Jewish disciple named Matthew was inspired by the Spirit of God to write a book. The finished product is what we know today as "The Gospel According to Matthew."

Nowhere in the four gospels do we find a single recorded word that Matthew spoke. Yet in his gospel, he gives us the words and works of Jesus Christ. The Holy Spirit used Matthew to accomplish three important tasks in the writing of his gospel.

First, it was a bridge builder. If a Bible reader were to jump from Malachi to Mark, or to Acts, or to Romans, he would be bewildered. Matthew's gospel is the bridge that leads us out of the Old Testament and into the New Testament.

Second, this book introduced a new King. Each of the four gospels has its own emphasis; Matthew's book is called "the gospel of the King." It was written primarily for Jewish readers. Being accustomed to keeping systematic records, Matthew gave us a beautifully organized account of our Lord's life and ministry.

Finally, the gospel introduced a new people. This new people, of course, was the church. Matthew was the only gospel writer to use the word *church* (Matt. 16:18; 18:17). The Greek word translated *church* means "a called-out assembly." In the New Testament, this refers to a local assembly of believers. Matthew made it clear that this new people, the church, must not maintain a racial or social exclusiveness. Faith in Jesus Christ makes believers "all one" in the body of Christ, the church.

## Ministering to Hearts

Matthew opened his heart to Jesus Christ and became a new person. This was not an easy decision for him to make. He was a native of Capernaum, and Capernaum had rejected the Lord (Matt. 11:23). Matthew was a well-known businessman in the city, and his old friends probably persecuted him.

Matthew not only opened his heart, but he also opened his home. He knew that most, if not all, of his old friends would drop him when he began to follow Jesus Christ, so Matthew took advantage of the situation and invited them all to meet Jesus.

Beyond even opening his heart and home, Matthew also opened his hands as he worked for Christ. According to tradition, Matthew ministered in Palestine for several years after the Lord's return to heaven and then made missionary journeys to the Jews who were dispersed among the Gentiles. The New Testament is silent on his life, but this we do know: Wherever the Scriptures travel in this world, the gospel written by Matthew continues to minister to hearts.

—*Warren W. Wiersbe*

# How to Use This Study

This study is designed for both individual and small-group use. We've divided it into eight lessons—each references one or more chapters in Warren W. Wiersbe's commentary *Be Loyal* (second edition, David C. Cook, 2008). While reading *Be Loyal* is not a prerequisite for going through this study, the additional insights and background Wiersbe offers can greatly enhance your study experience.

The **Getting Started** questions at the beginning of each lesson offer you an opportunity to record your first thoughts and reactions to the study text. This is an important step in the study process as those "first impressions" often include clues about what it is your heart is longing to discover.

The bulk of the study is found in the **Going Deeper** questions. These dive into the Bible text and, along with helpful excerpts from Wiersbe's commentary, help you examine not only the original context and meaning of the verses but also modern application.

**Looking Inward** narrows the focus down to your personal story. These intimate questions can be a bit uncomfortable at times, but don't shy away from honesty here. This is where you are asked to stand before the mirror of God's Word and look closely at what you see. It's the place to take a good look at yourself in light of the lesson and search for ways in which you can grow in faith.

**Going Forward** is the place where you can commit to paper those things you want or need to do in order to better live out the discoveries you made in the Looking Inward section. Don't skip or skim through this. Take the time to really consider what practical steps you might take to move closer to Christ. Then share your thoughts with a trusted friend who can act as an encourager and accountability partner.

Finally, there is a brief **Seeking Help** section to close the lesson. This is a reminder for you to invite God into your spiritual-growth process. If you choose to write out a prayer in this section, come back to it as you work through the lesson and continue to seek the Holy Spirit's guidance as you discover God's will for your life.

## Tips for Small Groups

A small group is a dynamic thing. One week it might seem like a group of close-knit friends. The next it might seem more like a group of uncomfortable strangers. A small-group leader's role is to read these subtle changes and adjust the tone of the discussion accordingly.

Small groups need to be safe places for people to talk openly. It is through shared wrestling with difficult life issues that some of the greatest personal growth is discovered. But in order for the group to feel safe, participants need to know it's okay *not* to share sometimes. Always invite honest disclosure, but never force someone to speak if he or she isn't comfortable doing so. (A savvy leader will follow up later with a group member who isn't comfortable sharing in a group setting to see if a one-on-one discussion is more appropriate.)

Have volunteers take turns reading excerpts from Scripture or from the commentary. The more each person is involved even in the mundane tasks, the more they'll feel comfortable opening up in more meaningful ways.

The leader should watch the clock and keep the discussion moving. Sometimes there may be more Going Deeper questions than your group can cover in your available time. If you've had a fruitful discussion, it's okay to move on without finishing everything. And if you think the group is getting bogged down on a question or has taken off on a tangent, you can simply say, "Let's go on to question 5." Be sure to save at least ten to fifteen minutes for the Going Forward questions.

Finally, soak your group meetings in prayer—before you begin, during as needed, and always at the end of your time together.

# Birth
## (MATTHEW 1—4)

*Before you begin ...*
- *Pray for the Holy Spirit to reveal truth and wisdom as you go through this lesson.*
- *Read Matthew 1—4. This lesson references chapters 2 and 3 in Be Loyal. It will be helpful for you to have your Bible and a copy of the commentary available as you work through this lesson.*

## Getting Started

### From the Commentary

If a man suddenly appears and claims to be a king, the public immediately asks for proof. What is his background? Who pays homage to him? What credentials can he present? Anticipating these important questions, Matthew opened his book with a careful account of the birth of Jesus Christ and the events that accompanied it.

—*Be Loyal,* page 25

1. What are the credentials of Jesus that Matthew presents in the first chapters of his gospel? Why would these have been of particular interest to the readers of his gospel?

2. Choose one verse or phrase from Matthew 1—4 that stands out to you. This could be something you're intrigued by, something that makes you uncomfortable, something that puzzles you, something that resonates with you, or just something you want to examine further. Write that here.

## Going Deeper

*From the Commentary*

> Matthew 1:16 and 1:18 make it clear that Jesus Christ's birth was different from that of any other Jewish boy named in the genealogy. Matthew pointed out that

Joseph did not "beget" Jesus Christ. Rather, Joseph was the "husband of Mary, of whom was born Jesus, who is called Christ." Jesus was born of an earthly mother without the need for an earthly father. This is known as the doctrine of the virgin birth.

—*Be Loyal*, page 26

3. Why is it important to the gospel story that Jesus was born of a virgin and had no earthly father? How might this distinction have been received by the Jews?

*More to Consider: To the Jewish people, betrothal (engagement) was equivalent to marriage—except that the man and woman did not live together. They were called husband and wife, and at the end of the engagement period, the marriage was consummated. How does this tradition play into Joseph and Mary's story? What does Joseph's response to Mary's pregnancy tell us about Joseph? About Mary? About God Himself?*

*From the Commentary*

> A person is identified not only by his friends, but also
> by his enemies. Herod pretended that he wanted to wor-
> ship the newborn King (Matt. 2:8), when in reality he
> wanted to destroy Him. God warned Joseph to take the
> child and Mary and flee to Egypt. Egypt was close. There
> were many Jews there, and the treasures received from
> the magi would more than pay the expenses for traveling
> and living there. But there was also another prophecy to
> fulfill, Hosea 11:1: "I called my Son out of Egypt."
>
> —*Be Loyal*, page 29

4. Why do you think Herod was afraid of a tiny baby? What does this say
about the way he ruled the land? About his confidence in his leadership?
About the power of the hopes and dreams of the Jewish people? How do
you see God's hand in Herod's role in this story?

*More to Consider: Magi were non-Jewish scholars who studied the stars. Though it is presumed (and often sung) that there were three magi, we really don't know how many there were. Why do you think God included the magi in the Christmas story? What were their roles? How was God glorified through their actions?*

## From Today's World

The wise men referenced in the Gospels were probably a lot like astrologers. Their calculations and presumptions would have been based on the movement and position of the stars. Today, astrology continues to have a strong influence in the lives of many who seek truth and wisdom about their lives and the world around them. Though many "astrology charts" are meant merely as entertainment, you'll find a large number of books in the philosophy and religion section of your local bookstore dedicated to the "science" of astrology.

5. What is the appeal of astrology? How did God use astrology to accomplish His plan at Jesus' birth? How was this different from an endorsement of astrology? In what ways does astrology contradict Christianity? What does this tell us about how we ought to consider astrology today?

*From the Commentary*

> Some thirty years passed between chapters 2 and 3 of
> Matthew, during which Jesus lived in Nazareth and
> worked as a carpenter (Matt. 13:55; Mark 6:3). But the
> time came for Him to begin His public ministry, which
> would culminate at the cross. Was He still qualified to
> be King? In chapters 3 and 4, Matthew assembled the
> testimonies of five witnesses to the person of Jesus Christ,
> that He is the Son of God and the King.
>
> The first of these is John the Baptist. For over four hundred
> years, the nation had not heard the voice of a prophet.
> Then John appeared and a great revival took place.
>
> —*Be Loyal*, page 35

6. Review Matthew 3:1–2, 7–10. What was the focus of John's preaching?
Why is this significant in the larger story? Where did John get his authority
to preach (3:3–4)? Why did John baptize Jesus? What was different about
this baptism (3:13–15)?

*From the Commentary*

> The coming of the Holy Spirit like a dove identified Jesus to John (John 1:31–34), and also assured Jesus as He began His ministry that the Spirit's ministry would always be His (John 3:34).
>
> —*Be Loyal*, page 37

7. Read Genesis 8:6–11. Why do you think a dove was used in this passage? What is the significance of the dove as a symbol for the Spirit in the book of Matthew?

*More to Consider: The name Jonah means "dove." In what ways did Jonah experience a baptism? What are some other similarities between Jonah's story and Jesus'?*

*From the Commentary*

> On three special occasions, the Father spoke from heaven:
> at Christ's baptism, at the Transfiguration (Matt. 17:3),
> and as Christ approached the cross (John 12:27–30).
>
> The Father's statement from heaven seems to be an echo
> of Psalm 2:7—"The Lord hath said unto me, 'Thou art my
> Son; this day have I begotten thee.'" Acts 13:33 informs
> us that this "begetting" refers to His resurrection from
> the dead and not to His birth at Bethlehem.
>
> But the Father's statement also relates Jesus Christ to the
> "Suffering Servant" prophesied in Isaiah 40—53.
>
> —*Be Loyal*, pages 37–38

8. What did God say to Jesus at His baptism? In what ways is this like Psalm
2:7? What is the significance of the similarity? How does this statement
also relate to the Isaiah passages? Why is this important to the gospel story?

*From the Commentary*

> From the high and holy experience of blessing at the Jordan, Jesus was led into the wilderness for testing. Jesus was not tempted so that the Father could learn anything about His Son, for the Father had already given Jesus His divine approval. Jesus was tempted so that every creature in heaven, on earth, and under the earth might know that Jesus Christ is the Conqueror. He exposed Satan and his tactics, and He defeated Satan.
>
> —*Be Loyal*, page 38

9. What were the three temptations Satan offered (Matt. 4:1–11)? What was the purpose of each temptation? What did Jesus prove through each of these temptations? Why is it important that Jesus exposed Satan and his tactics?

*From the Commentary*

> Matthew has already shown us that every detail of our Lord's life was controlled by the Word of God. Remember that between the end of His temptation and the statement in Matthew 4:12 comes the ministry described in John

1:19 through John 3:36. We must not think that John the Baptist was thrown into prison immediately after our Lord's temptation. Matthew wrote his book *topically* rather than *chronologically*.

But Jesus not only proclaimed the good news and taught the people God's truth, He also called to Himself a few disciples whom He could train for the work of the kingdom. In Matthew 4:17–22, we read of the call of Peter, Andrew, James, and John, men who had already met Jesus and trusted Him (John 1:29–42).

—*Be Loyal*, pages 41, 43

10. Why do you think Jesus chose to call disciples after He'd already been in ministry for a time? What is significant about the role of the disciples? Why would Jesus call fishermen? What character traits would they have that might benefit Jesus' ministry?

## Looking Inward

Take a moment to reflect on all that you've explored thus far in this study of Matthew 1—4. Review your notes and answers and think about how each of these things matters in your life today.

*Tips for Small Groups: To get the most out of this section, form pairs or trios and have group members take turns answering these questions. Be honest and as open as you can in this discussion, but most of all, be encouraging and supportive of others. Be sensitive to those who are going through particularly difficult times and don't press for people to speak if they're uncomfortable doing so.*

11. What is the most surprising thing to you about God's decision to send Jesus as a baby? How does this aspect of the gospel story affect the manner in which you share Christ with others?

12. What captured you most about Jesus' temptations in the wilderness? In what ways does this help you relate personally to Christ? How have you faced temptations? What was your response to those temptations? What does Jesus' victory over Satan tell you about God's power in Jesus' life? About the power available to you today?

13. In what ways are you like or unlike the fishermen Jesus chose as His disciples? What character traits do you have that make you a prime candidate for being a disciple? What are some areas for improvement? In what ways are you already living out your life as Jesus' disciple?

## Going Forward

14. Think of one or two things that you have learned that you'd like to work on in the coming week. Remember that this is all about quality, not quantity. It's better to work on one specific area of life and do it well than to work on many and do poorly (or to be so overwhelmed that you simply don't try).

Do you need to further explore the reason God sent Jesus as a baby? Do you need to discover the power over temptation that God gave Jesus in the wilderness? Be specific. Go back through Matthew 1—4 and put a

star next to the phrase or verse that is most encouraging to you. Consider memorizing this verse.

*Real-Life Application Ideas: Hold a special Christmas celebration no matter what time of the year it is. But instead of the traditional trappings, consider a celebration that focuses solely on the great mystery of God coming to the earth in human form, as a baby. Use the event to contemplate the richness and creativity of a God who so loved us that He became like us. Use your own creativity to come up with a party or celebration that expresses thankfulness for God's greatest gift.*

## Seeking Help

15. Write a prayer below (or simply pray one in silence), inviting God to work on your mind and heart in those areas you've previously noted. Be honest about your desires and fears.

*Notes for Small Groups:*

- *Look for ways to put into practice the things you wrote in the Going Forward section. Talk with other group members about your ideas and commit to being accountable to one another.*

- *During the coming week, ask the Holy Spirit to continue to reveal truth to you from what you've read and studied.*

- *Before you start the next lesson, read Matthew 5—7. For more in-depth lesson preparation, read chapters 4–6 in* Be Loyal.

# Principles
## (MATTHEW 5—7)

*Before you begin …*
- *Pray for the Holy Spirit to reveal truth and wisdom as you go through this lesson.*
- *Read Matthew 5—7. This lesson references chapters 4–6 in* Be Loyal. *It will be helpful for you to have your Bible and a copy of the commentary available as you work through this lesson.*

## Getting Started

*From the Commentary*

The Sermon on the Mount is one of the most misunderstood messages that Jesus ever gave. One group says it is God's plan of salvation, that if we ever hope to go to heaven we must obey these rules. Another group calls it a "charter for world peace" and begs the nations of the earth to accept it. Still a third group tells us that the Sermon on the Mount does not apply to today, but that it will apply at some future time, perhaps during the tribulation or the millennial kingdom.

I have always felt that Matthew 5:20 was the key to this important sermon: "For I say unto you, that except your righteousness shall exceed the righteousness of the scribes and Pharisees, ye shall in no case enter into the kingdom of heaven." The main theme is true righteousness. The religious leaders had an artificial, external righteousness based on law. But the righteousness Jesus described is a true and vital righteousness that begins internally, in the heart. The Pharisees were concerned about the minute details of conduct, but they neglected the major matter of *character*. Conduct flows out of character.

—*Be Loyal,* page 45

1. What was your initial impression of the Sermon on the Mount? Why do you think people have interpreted this important message in so many diverse ways? What are the core truths you glean from the sermon?

*More to Consider: The Beatitudes describe the attitudes that ought to be in our lives today. Review Matthew 5:3, 4–6, 7–9, and 10–16. How would you describe the attitudes discussed in these passages?*

2. Choose one verse or phrase from Matthew 5—7 that stands out to you. This could be something you're intrigued by, something that makes you uncomfortable, something that puzzles you, something that resonates with you, or just something you want to examine further. Write that here.

## Going Deeper

*From the Commentary*

> Jesus took six important Old Testament laws and interpreted them for His people in the light of the new life He came to give. He made a fundamental change without altering God's standards: He dealt with the attitudes and intents of the heart and not simply with the external action.
>
> The six laws:
>
> Murder (Matt. 5:21–26; Ex. 20:13)

Adultery (Matt. 5:27–30; Ex. 20:14)

Divorce (Matt. 5:31–32) [This will be dealt with more in a later chapter]

Swearing (Matt. 5:33–37; Lev. 19:12; Deut. 23:23)

Retaliation (Matt. 5:38–42; Lev. 24:19–22)

Love of enemies (Matt. 5:43–48; Lev. 19:17–18)

—*Be Loyal*, pages 50–53

3. Review each of the Scripture passages noted above. How does Jesus reinterpret each of these laws? How might the teachers of the law have responded to Jesus' reinterpretations? What does this tell us about Jesus' ministry? About God's intent for the law before Jesus, and after?

## From the Commentary

The true righteousness of the kingdom must be applied in the everyday activities of life. This is the emphasis in the rest of the Sermon on the Mount. Jesus related this principle to our relationships to God in worship (Matt. 6:1–18), our relationship to material things (Matt. 6:19–34), and our relationship to other people (Matt. 7:1–20).

Jesus also warned about the danger of hypocrisy (Matt. 6:2, 5, 16), the sin of using religion to cover up sin. A hypocrite is not a person who falls short of his high ideals, or who occasionally sins, because all of us experience these failures. A hypocrite *deliberately* uses religion to cover up his sins and promote his own gains. The Greek word translated *hypocrite* originally meant "an actor who wears a mask."

—*Be Loyal*, page 55

4. What are the key statements in Matthew 6—7 that teach about our relationship with God? With material things? With our relationship to other people? Circle these. Why does Jesus focus on the danger of hypocrisy in the context of these teachings? How does each of these things apply to today's Christian? (Give specific examples.)

## From Today's World

In a commerce-driven society like the United States, sometimes Christianity gets caught between ministry and business. Setting aside the misuses of Christianity or religion for person gain, there remain plenty of challenges for any Christian business or ministry to "make it," especially as competition for the consumer's dollars becomes even greater, such as when the economy is in a difficult season. Some ministries and businesses have to make the difficult decision to close shop amid difficult times, while others choose to expand their influence by becoming more mainstream.

5. How does a Christian business or ministry thrive in difficult times without becoming hypocritical in its business model? Is it possible for Christian businesses and ministries to continue if they are not financially successful? What determines the "success" of a business or ministry, according to the teaching Jesus offers in the Sermon on the Mount?

## From the Commentary

In Matthew 6:5–15, Jesus gave four instructions to guide us in our praying.

We must pray in secret before we pray in public (v. 6).

We must pray sincerely (vv. 7–8).

We must pray in God's will (vv. 9–13).

We must pray, having a forgiving spirit toward others (vv. 14–15).

—*Be Loyal*, pages 56–58

6. Review Matthew 6:5–15. What are the practical implications of Jesus' teaching on prayer? How is this to be lived out in the life of the church? In the life of the individual? Why do you think Jesus gives such attention to prayer? What does this say about the role of prayer in the life of a believer?

*From the Commentary*

We are accustomed to dividing life into the "spiritual" and the "material"; but Jesus made no such division. In many of His parables, He made it clear that a right attitude toward wealth is a mark of true spirituality (see Luke 12:13ff.; 16:1–31). The Pharisees were covetous (Luke 16:14) and used religion to make money. If we have the true righteousness of Christ in our lives, then we will have a proper attitude toward material wealth.

Nowhere did Jesus magnify poverty or criticize the legitimate getting of wealth. God made all things, including food, clothing, and precious metals. God has declared that all things He has made are good (Gen. 1:31). God knows that we need certain things in order to live (Matt. 6:32). In fact, He has given us "richly all things to enjoy" (1 Tim. 6:17). It is not wrong to possess things, *but it is wrong for things to possess us.*

—*Be Loyal*, page 60

7. Why do many people tend to separate the "spiritual" from the "material"? How does Jesus directly attack this wrong philosophy in Matthew 6:19–34? In what ways are people often possessed by the things they own? What are the clues that tell us if someone is possessed by his possessions? What are the actions that must be taken to avoid being possessed by material things?

*More to Consider: Review the following passages that speak to the idea of covetousness: Exodus 20:17; Psalms 119:36; Mark 7:22–23; Luke 12:15–21; Ephesians 5:5; Colossians 3:5. How does each of these passages line up with Jesus' teaching in Matthew 6?*

## From the Commentary

The scribes and Pharisees were guilty of exercising a false judgment about themselves, other people, and even the Lord. Their false righteousness helped to encourage this false judgment. This explains why our Lord closed this important sermon with a discussion of judgment. In it He discussed three judgments.

The first principle of judgment is that we begin with ourselves. Jesus did not forbid us to judge others, for careful discrimination is essential in the Christian life. Christian love is not blind (Phil. 1:9–10). The person who believes all that he hears and accepts everyone who claims to be spiritual will experience confusion and great spiritual loss. But before we judge others, we must judge ourselves.

—*Be Loyal*, page 65

8. What does it mean to judge ourselves first? (See Matt. 7:1–5.) What are examples of the false judgment Jesus warns against in 7:3–5? What does true judgment of others involve (7:15–19)?

## From the Commentary

Second, Christians must exercise discernment, for not everyone is a sheep. Some people are dogs or hogs, and some are wolves in sheep's clothing! We are the Lord's sheep, but this does not mean we should let people pull the wool over our eyes!

As God's people, we are privileged to handle the "holy things" of the Lord. He has entrusted to us the precious truths of the Word of God (2 Cor. 4:7), and we must regard them carefully.

*—Be Loyal*, page 67

9. According to Matthew 7:7–11, what tools are Christians given to help us be wise discerners of truth and not inappropriately judgmental? What is the guiding principle of judging (7:12), and how does this principle help us make good judgments? In what ways has this statement been misinterpreted?

*From the Commentary*

> From picturing two ways and two trees, our Lord closed
> His message by picturing two builders and their houses.
> The two ways illustrate the *start* of the life of faith; the
> two trees illustrate the *growth* and results of the life of
> faith here and now; and the two houses illustrate the *end*
> of this life of faith, when God shall call everything to
> judgment. There are false prophets at the gate that leads
> to the broad way, making it easy for people to enter. But
> at the end of the way, there is destruction. The final test is
> not what we think of ourselves, or what others may think.
> The final test is: *What will God say?*
>
> —*Be Loyal*, page 70

10. How can Christians prepare for this final judgment? What answer does
Jesus give in the Sermon on the Mount? How do Christians pursue true
righteousness?

## Looking Inward

Take a moment to reflect on all that you've explored thus far in this study
of Matthew 5—7. Review your notes and answers and think about how
each of these things matters in your life today.

*Tips for Small Groups: To get the most out of this section, form pairs or trios and have group members take turns answering these questions. Be honest and as open as you can in this discussion, but most of all, be encouraging and supportive of others. Be sensitive to those who are going through particularly difficult times and don't press for people to speak if they're uncomfortable doing so.*

11. How are you doing in your relationships with others, material things, and God, according to Jesus' teaching in Matthew 5—7? What are some areas in need of improvement? What are practical steps you can take to help you grow more Christlike in these relationships?

12. In what ways do you tend to separate the spiritual from the material? Why is it tempting to do this? How can you integrate these two things in a way that is pleasing to God? What changes would you have to make in your daily life to do this?

13. In what ways do you tend to judge others inappropriately? How do you know when you're using biblical discernment instead of self-serving judgment? What does it take to present yourself worthy to God in the final judgment? How does your life reflect, in practical ways, a decision to pursue Christlikeness above all else?

## Going Forward

14. Think of one or two things that you have learned that you'd like to work on in the coming week. Remember that this is all about quality, not quantity. It's better to work on one specific area of life and do it well than to work on many and do poorly (or to be so overwhelmed that you simply don't try).

Do you need to address your relationship to material things? Do you need to deal with a judgmental attitude toward someone, or grow more discerning about someone else? Be specific. Go back through Matthew 5—7 and put a star next to the phrase or verse that is most encouraging to you. Consider memorizing this verse.

*Real-Life Application Ideas: Take a personal inventory of the material aspects of your life—everything from your family to your job. Examine each one in light of the spiritual truths Jesus teaches about in Matthew 5—7. If you find a disconnect between the material and the spiritual, talk with a wise friend about how to solve this. Then put that plan into action.*

## Seeking Help

15. Write a prayer below (or simply pray one in silence), inviting God to work on your mind and heart in those areas you've previously noted. Be honest about your desires and fears.

*Notes for Small Groups:*

- *Look for ways to put into practice the things you wrote in the Going Forward section. Talk with other group members about your ideas and commit to being accountable to one another.*

- *During the coming week, ask the Holy Spirit to continue to reveal truth to you from what you've read and studied.*

- *Before you start the next lesson, read Matthew 8—10. For more in-depth lesson preparation, read chapters 7–8 in* Be Loyal.

# Power
## (MATTHEW 8—10)

*Before you begin ...*
- *Pray for the Holy Spirit to reveal truth and wisdom as you go through this lesson.*
- *Read Matthew 8—10. This lesson references chapters 7–8 in Be Loyal. It will be helpful for you to have your Bible and a copy of the commentary available as you work through this lesson.*

## Getting Started

### From the Commentary

Certainly our Lord's miracles were additional credentials to prove His claim as the Messiah of Israel. "The Jews require a sign" (1 Cor. 1:22). While miracles of themselves are not proof that a man has been sent by God (even Satan can perform miracles [2 Thess. 2:9]), they do add weight to his claim, especially if his character and conduct are godly. In the case of Jesus Christ, His miracles also fulfilled Old Testament prophecies (see

Isa. 29:18–19; 35:4–6). Matthew 8:17 refers us to Isaiah 53:4, and Jesus Himself in Matthew 11:1–5 referred John the Baptist to the Old Testament promises. These same "signs and wonders" would be the credentials of His followers in their ministries (Matt. 10:8; Heb. 2:1–4).

Along with His compassion and credentials, there was a third reason for miracles: His concern to reveal saving truth to people. The miracles were "sermons in action."

*—Be Loyal,* pages 75–76

1. What is it about miracles that adds credence to Jesus' claim as Messiah? What do we learn about Jesus' character from the sorts of miracles He performed? What do we learn about God Himself? In what ways were Jesus' miracles "sermons in action"?

*More to Consider: Jesus didn't perform miracles to gain a following or draw a crowd. More often than not, he avoided the crowd. And there are even times when he instructed those whom He had healed not to talk too much about it (Matt. 8:4; 9:30; Luke 8:56). Why would Jesus want to keep the news of His miracles quiet?*

2. Choose one verse or phrase from Matthew 8—10 that stands out to you. This could be something you're intrigued by, something that makes you uncomfortable, something that puzzles you, something that resonates with you, or just something you want to examine further. Write that here.

## Going Deeper

*From the Commentary*

> Lepers, Gentiles, and women were considered outcasts by many Jewish people, especially the Pharisees. Many Pharisees would pray each morning, "I give thanks that I am a man and not a woman, a Jew and not a Gentile, a freeman and not a slave."
>
> But Jesus gave grace to the outcasts. There are many examples of this in Matthew, including:
>
> Jesus cleanses a leper (Matt. 8:1–4).
>
> Jesus heals a centurion's servant (Matt. 8:5–13).
>
> Jesus heals Peter's mother-in-law (Matt. 8:14–17).
>
> —*Be Loyal*, pages 76–78

3. Review Matthew 8:1–17 and the miracles Jesus performed. Why is each of these significant in light of the Pharisees' disdain for outcasts? What do these miracles teach us about Jesus? About how we are to relate to those our society might deem outcasts?

*More to Consider: Matthew 8:18–22 could be described as a "discipleship" interlude. It marks the first time Jesus is referred to as "Son of Man." Why is this particular title significant to Jesus' ministry? How would such a title have been received by those seeking a Messiah? How would it have been received by the Pharisees and others who doubted Jesus' claims?*

## From the Commentary

The persons involved in the miracles recorded in Matthew 8:23—9:8 all had a need for peace, and Jesus provided that peace.

The three miracles are:

Peace in the storm (8:23–27). The Sea of Galilee is about

thirteen miles long and eight miles wide. It was not unusual for violent storms suddenly to sweep across the water. Jesus undoubtedly knew the storm was coming and certainly could have prevented it. But He permitted it that He might teach His disciples some lessons.

Peace in a community (8:28–34). This dramatic incident is most revealing. It shows what *Satan* does for a man: robs him of sanity and self-control; fills him with fears; robs him of the joys of home and friends; and (if possible) condemns him to an eternity of judgment. It also reveals what *society* does for a man in need: restrains him, isolates him, threatens him, but society is unable to change him. See, then, what Jesus Christ can do for a man whose whole life—within and without—is bondage and battle.

Peace in the conscience (9:1–8). The Lord had shown Himself powerful over sickness and storms, but what could He do about *sin?* Palsy was a gradual paralysis. This man was unable to help himself, but fortunately he had four friends with love, faith, and hope. They brought him to Jesus and permitted nothing to stand in their way. Was the man's physical condition the result of his sin? We do not know. But we do know that Jesus dealt with the sin problem first, for this is always the greatest need.

—*Be Loyal*, pages 79–80

4. In what ways did Jesus offer peace through the three miracles in Matthew 8:23—9:8? What message did this give to Jesus' early

followers? What message does it provide for Christians today? Why is peace such a much-needed thing in today's society? What are the things that challenge peace today?

## From Today's World

There is an ongoing debate both within and without the church about the existence of modern miracles. While some claim evidence for healing that is being performed today, others challenge those claims or offer alternative explanations for these medical "miracles." Whatever your opinion on the more visible proclamations of healing (faith healers on television, for example), there certainly are stories that defy easy scientific explanation. Are these examples of modern miracles? Or merely as-yet-unexplained coincidences?

5. Why do you think there are fewer (if any) miracles being performed today, whereas Scripture tells of many miracles performed not only by Jesus, but also by his disciples? Does the existence or nonexistence of miracles affect the importance or truth of Christian faith? Explain. How would modern miracles affect the faith lives of believers? The lives of nonbelievers? If you've known or heard of a miracle, what were the circumstances of that event?

*From the Commentary*

In Matthew 9:18–38, Matthew recorded four miracles dealing with restoration.

A broken home (vv. 18–19, 23–26). When Jairus first came to Jesus, his daughter was close to death. The delay caused by the healing of the woman gave "the last enemy" opportunity to do its work. The ruler's friends came and told him that his daughter had died.

A broken hope (vv. 20–22). Mark 5:26 informs us that this woman had tried many physicians, but none could help her. Imagine the despair and discouragement she felt. Her hopes were shattered.

Broken vision (vv. 27–34). We are not told why these men were blind. Blindness was a serious problem in the East in that day. The records state that Jesus healed at least six blind men, and each case was different.

A broken spirit (vv. 32–34). The final miracle in this series involved a demon. While there is a difference between sicknesses and demonic workings (Matt. 10:8), the demons do have the power to cause physical afflictions. In this case, the demon made the man mute.

—*Be Loyal*, pages 81–83

6. What are the common threads in the miracles Jesus performed in Matthew 9:18–38? In what ways were each of these people restored? What restoration do people need today? How can they find that restoration?

## From the Commentary

> The work of salvation could be accomplished only by Jesus Christ, and He did it alone. But the *witness* of this salvation could only be accomplished by His people, those who have trusted Him and been saved. The King needed ambassadors to carry the message—and He *still* needs them. "Whom shall I send, and who will go for us?" (Isa. 6:8). It is not enough that we *pray* for laborers (Matt. 9:36–38). We must also make ourselves available to serve Him.
>
> Before Jesus sent His ambassadors out to minister, He preached an "ordination sermon" to encourage and prepare them. In this sermon, the King had something to say to *all* of His servants—past, present, and future. Unless we recognize this fact, the message of Matthew 10 will seem hopelessly confused.
>
> —*Be Loyal*, page 85

7. How did Jesus prepare His ambassadors for ministry? Circle the specific teaching in chapter 10 that applies not only to the ambassadors Jesus was preparing in His time, but also for us today. In your experience with the church, where do you see this sort of preparation happening?

*More to Consider: Jesus had many disciples, some of whom were merely hangers-on and some who were truly converted (see John 6:66). But out of that group, He selected a smaller group of twelve He called apostles. This word comes from the Greek word* apostello, *which means to "send forth with a commission." Why did Jesus entrust the commission to such a small group? What does this suggest to us today about ministry and leadership?*

### From the Commentary

Christ's commission to these twelve men is not our commission today. He sent them only to the people of Israel. "To the Jew first" is the historic pattern, for "salvation is of the Jews" (John 4:22). These twelve ambassadors announced the coming of the kingdom just as John the Baptist had done (Matt. 3:2) and Jesus Himself (Matt. 4:17). Sad to say, the nation rejected both Christ and

His ambassadors, and the kingdom was taken from them (Matt. 21:43).

—*Be Loyal*, page 86

8. Why is it significant that the apostles' mission was different from ours today? What does this say about God's plan for salvation? In what ways do Christ's ambassadors today face rejection from the people they are called to reach?

## From the Commentary

The "atmosphere" of Matthew 10:16–23 is different from that in the previous section. Here the Lord spoke of persecution, but we have no record that the Twelve suffered during their tour. Jesus also spoke of a ministry to the Gentiles (Matt. 10:18). The Holy Spirit had not yet been given, yet Jesus talked about the Spirit speaking in them (Matt. 10:20). Matthew 10:22 seems to indicate a worldwide persecution, yet the apostles were ministering only in their own land. Finally, Matthew 10:23 speaks about the return of the Lord, which certainly moves these events into the future.

—*Be Loyal*, page 87

9. In what ways does this passage seem to speak to future ambassadors of Christ? How might Jesus' words in this section have been received by the early disciples? What implications did these words have for their future ministries? What do they say to us today?

## From the Commentary

> While the truths in Matthew 10:24–42 would apply to God's servants during any period of Bible history, they seem to have a special significance for the church today. The emphasis is, "Fear not!" (Matt. 10:26, 28, 31). Several reasons show why we must not be afraid to openly confess Christ. Here are some reasons found in Matthew 10:
>
> Suffering is to be expected (vv. 24–25).
>
> God will bring everything to light (vv. 26–27).
>
> We fear God alone (v. 28).
>
> God cares for His own (vv. 29–31).
>
> Christ honors those who confess Him (vv. 32–33).
>
> We cannot escape conflict (vv. 34–39).
>
> We can be a blessing to others (vv. 40–42).
>
> —*Be Loyal*, pages 89–92

10. Review each of the reasons we ought not to fear as noted above and found in Matthew 10:24–42. How is each of these reasons applicable today? What are some examples of the conflict that we face when living as Christ's disciples? How does being a blessing to others give us reason not to fear?

## Looking Inward

Take a moment to reflect on all that you've explored thus far in this study of Matthew 8—10. Review your notes and answers and think about how each of these things matters in your life today.

*Tips for Small Groups: To get the most out of this section, form pairs or trios and have group members take turns answering these questions. Be honest and as open as you can in this discussion, but most of all, be encouraging and supportive of others. Be sensitive to those who are going through particularly difficult times and don't press for people to speak if they're uncomfortable doing so.*

11. What is your reaction to Jesus' miracles as recorded in Matthew 8—9? Do you believe there are modern miracles today? Why or why not? What sorts of restoration do you long for in your life? In the lives of your loved ones?

12. In what ways are you living out your role as a modern disciple? How is your role similar to that of the Twelve? How is it different? What lessons can you learn from Matthew 10 to help you be a better disciple?

13. Describe a time when you were afraid to share your faith in Christ. What causes you to be fearful about confessing Christ? How can the message of Matthew 10 help reduce those fears?

## Going Forward

14. Think of one or two things that you have learned that you'd like to work on in the coming week. Remember that this is all about quality, not quantity. It's better to work on one specific area of life and do it well than to work on many and do poorly (or to be so overwhelmed that you simply don't try).

Do you want to pray for restoration for yourself or someone else? Do you need to overcome fears of sharing your faith? Be specific. Go back through Matthew 8—10 and put a star next to the phrase or verse that is most encouraging to you. Consider memorizing this verse.

*Real-Life Application Ideas: Challenge your fears of confessing Christ by making a specific, measurable plan to tell at least one person you know about your faith in the coming week. Keep in mind that the best way to share is in the context of an existing friendship, but don't be blind to other opportunities God might give you as you seek to share the gospel.*

## Seeking Help

15. Write a prayer below (or simply pray one in silence), inviting God to work on your mind and heart in those areas you've previously noted. Be honest about your desires and fears.

*Notes for Small Groups:*

- *Look for ways to put into practice the things you wrote in the Going Forward section. Talk with other group members about your ideas and commit to being accountable to one another.*

- *During the coming week, ask the Holy Spirit to continue to reveal truth to you from what you've read and studied.*

- *Before you start the next lesson, read Matthew 11—13. For more in-depth lesson preparation, read chapters 9–10 in* Be Loyal.

# Conflict and Secrets
## (MATTHEW 11—13)

*Before you begin …*

- *Pray for the Holy Spirit to reveal truth and wisdom as you go through this lesson.*
- *Read Matthew 11—13. This lesson references chapters 9–10 in* Be Loyal. *It will be helpful for you to have your Bible and a copy of the commentary available as you work through this lesson.*

## Getting Started

### From the Commentary

John the Baptist was in prison in the fortress of Machaerus because he had courageously denounced the adulterous marriage of Herod Antipas and Herodias (Luke 3:19–20). It seems that the Jewish leaders would have opposed Herod and sought to free John, but they did nothing. Their attitude toward John reflected their feeling toward Jesus, for John had pointed to Jesus and honored Him.

It is not difficult to sympathize with John as he suffered in prison. He was a man of the desert, yet he was confined indoors. He was an active man, with a divine mandate to preach, yet he was silenced. He had announced judgment, and yet that judgment was slow in coming (Matt. 3:7–12). He received only partial reports of Jesus' ministry and could not see the total picture.

—*Be Loyal,* page 95

1. Read Matthew 11:2–6. Why do you think John asked Jesus this question? What does Jesus' reply reveal about His relationship to John?

*More to Consider: Who are the "wise and learned" Jesus refers to in Matthew 11:25? Why do you think they rejected John and Jesus?*

2. Choose one verse or phrase from Matthew 11—13 that stands out to you. This could be something you're intrigued by, something that makes you uncomfortable, something that puzzles you, something that resonates with you, or just something you want to examine further. Write that here.

# Going Deeper

*From the Commentary*

> Jesus deliberately violated the Sabbath traditions on several occasions. He had taught the people that mere external laws could never save them or make them holy; true righteousness had to come from the heart. The Hebrew word *sabat* means "repose or rest," which explains why Matthew introduced these Sabbath conflicts at this point. Jesus offers rest to all who will come to Him; there is no rest in mere religious observances.
>
> It was lawful to satisfy your hunger from your neighbor's field (Deut. 23:24–25). But to do it on the Sabbath was a breach of the law according to the traditions of the scribes and Pharisees, for it meant doing work. Jesus gave a three-fold reply to their accusation.
>
> He appealed to a king (vv. 3–4).
>
> He appealed to the priests (vv. 5–6).
>
> He appealed to a prophet (v. 7).
>
> —*Be Loyal*, page 98

3. What is significant about Jesus' threefold reply to the Pharisees? What questions or concerns would each of Jesus' appeals have answered? What does this tell us about the opposition Jesus was beginning to face? About how Jesus intended to respond to challenges presented by the Pharisees?

## From the Commentary

> When the leaders rejected John the Baptist, they were rejecting *the Father* who sent him. When they rejected Jesus, they were rejecting *the Son*. But when they rejected the ministry of the apostles, they rejected *the Holy Spirit*—and that is the end. There is no more witness. Such rejection cannot be forgiven.
>
> The phrase "idle word" in Matthew 12:36 means "words that accomplish nothing." If God is going to judge our "small talk," how much more will He judge our deliberate words? It is by our conversation *at unguarded moments* that we reveal our true character.
>
> *—Be Loyal,* page 101

4. What are the "careless words" ("idle words") that the scribes and Pharisees were speaking? What are some examples of careless words we speak within the church today? How do the words spoken when "no one is watching" define our character?

## From the Commentary

> "The Jews require a sign" (1 Cor. 1:22). To ask for a sign
> was evidence of unbelief: They wanted Him to *prove* that
> He was the Messiah.
>
> Jesus gave three responses to their challenge.
>
> He reviewed their history (vv. 39–42).
>
> He revealed their hearts (vv. 43–45).
>
> He rejected their honor (vv. 46–50).
>
> —*Be Loyal*, pages 102–4

5. Why did the Jewish leaders demand a sign from Jesus? Why didn't Jesus
give them one in the way they demanded? What did Jesus' answers reveal
about the accusers? About Jesus Himself?

## From the History Books

Jesus wasn't the only person who claimed to be the Messiah. A few Jews
who preceded Jesus' birth made that claim, as did many more who came
after Jesus' birth, death, and resurrection. Additionally, many people have

claimed to be the second coming of Christ, including Sun Myung Moon, founder of the Unification Church, and cult leader David Koresh, leader of the ill-fated Branch Davidians.

6. Why do you think so many people have claimed to be the Messiah? What evidence do we have today that disproves their claims? What makes Jesus' claims unique? How is Jesus' response to those who challenged His Messiahship further evidence that He was the one true Messiah?

*More to Consider: The word* parable *means "to cast alongside." It is a story, or comparison, that is put alongside something else to help make the lesson clear. Jesus used parables to teach a variety of lessons. In this section of Matthew, He teaches about the kingdom of God. Why might parables have been a good choice for teaching about God's kingdom?*

## From the Commentary

Chapter 13 records the events of a crisis day in the ministry of Jesus Christ. He knew that the growing opposition of the religious leaders would lead to His crucifixion. This fact He had to explain to His disciples. But their logical question would be, "What will happen to the kingdom about which we have been preaching?" That question is answered in this series of parables. So, He first explained the truth concerning the kingdom, and then later explained to them the facts about the cross.

—*Be Loyal*, page 107

7. Why did Jesus speak in parables instead of stating things clearly and simply? Who was responsible for the deafness and blindness of those who ignored His teaching? What is the significance of Jesus' answer (v. 11) to the question in Matthew 13:10? How might this have been received by the perplexed disciples?

## From the Commentary

The parable of the sower does not begin with "The kingdom of heaven is like" because it describes how the kingdom begins. It begins with the preaching of the Word, the planting of the seed in the hearts of people. When we say, "Let me plant this thought in your mind," we express the idea of this parable. The seed is God's Word; the various soils represent different kinds of hearts; and the varied results show the different responses to the Word of God. Jesus explained this parable so there is no doubt of its meaning.

—*Be Loyal*, page 108

8. How is God's Word like seed? (See Heb. 4:12.) Why is the metaphor of soils particularly appropriate to describe the variety of responses to God's Word? Underline Jesus' explanation of the parable. Why do you think Jesus chose to privately explain this particular parable and not others?

*More to Consider: In an agrarian culture like that of Jesus' day, the metaphor of seed planting would have been particularly apropos and understandable. What are some modern metaphors that could have the same sort of understandability and immediacy?*

## From the Commentary

> Satan opposes the kingdom by trying to snatch the Word from hearts (Matt. 13:4, 19). But when that fails, he has other ways of attacking God's work. These three parables reveal that Satan is primarily an *imitator*: He plants false Christians, he encourages a false growth, and he introduces false doctrine.
>
> —*Be Loyal*, page 109

9. Read Matthew 13:24–43. How does each of these parables speak to Satan's role in opposing the kingdom? What warnings do these parables offer Christians? In what ways do you see evidence of these dangers in today's culture? According to Jesus' parables, what are the practical responses Christians ought to have to these dangers?

## From the Commentary

> When Jesus finished these parables, He went across the sea in a storm and delivered the demoniacs in the country of the Gadarenes. Matthew recorded this in 8:28–34. It

was then that Jesus went to His hometown of Nazareth, and this event Matthew recorded in 13:53–58.

Two things amazed the people of Nazareth: the Lord's words and His works. However, they did not trust in Him, and this limited His ministry.

—*Be Loyal*, page 115

10. Why didn't the people of Jesus' hometown trust in Him? What unique challenges did Jesus face in presenting His ministry to people who had watched Him grow up?

## Looking Inward

Take a moment to reflect on all that you've explored thus far in this study of Matthew 11—13. Review your notes and answers and think about how each of these things matters in your life today.

*Tips for Small Groups: To get the most out of this section, form pairs or trios and have group members take turns answering these questions. Be honest and as open as you can in this discussion, but most of all, be encouraging and supportive of others. Be sensitive to those who are going through particularly difficult times and don't press for people to speak if they're uncomfortable doing so.*

11. Jesus had a ready answer for the scribes and Pharisees who often challenged Him. He went right to the Scriptures and tradition to answer their questions. How prepared are you to answer challenges to your beliefs? What are some things you might do to better prepare yourself for attacks on your faith?

12. What was your initial reaction to Jesus' explanation of why He speaks in parables? Which of Jesus' parables do you find the most compelling? The most confusing? What is it about stories and metaphors that makes them a great tool for teaching? What are some of the stories you remember from childhood that still influence how you live your life?

13. What appeals to you most about the kingdom of God that Jesus describes in Matthew 13? What questions do you have as you examine Jesus' teachings here? What implications do Jesus' lessons have for how we are to live today?

## Going Forward

14. Think of one or two things that you have learned that you'd like to work on in the coming week. Remember that this is all about quality, not quantity. It's better to work on one specific area of life and do it well than to work on many and do poorly (or to be so overwhelmed that you simply don't try).

Do you need to be better prepared to answer questions about your faith? Do you need to reflect on what kind of soil your heart is for receiving the Word? Be specific. Go back through Matthew 11—13 and put a

star next to the phrase or verse that is most encouraging to you. Consider memorizing this verse.

*Real-Life Application Ideas: Go online and explore the parable-storytelling technique and how it's been used over the years. Then write your own parable to describe an aspect of the Christian life today. After you've finished your parable, test it on a few friends to see how successful you were at sharing the message.*

## Seeking Help

15. Write a prayer below (or simply pray one in silence), inviting God to work on your mind and heart in those areas you've previously noted. Be honest about your desires and fears.

*Notes for Small Groups:*

- *Look for ways to put into practice the things you wrote in the Going Forward section. Talk with other group members about your ideas and commit to being accountable to one another.*

- *During the coming week, ask the Holy Spirit to continue to reveal truth to you from what you've read and studied.*

- *Before you start the next lesson, read Matthew 14—15. For more in-depth lesson preparation, read chapters 11–12 in* Be Loyal.

# Concern
## (MATTHEW 14—15)

*Before you begin ...*

- *Pray for the Holy Spirit to reveal truth and wisdom as you go through this lesson.*
- *Read Matthew 14—15. This lesson references chapters 11–12 in* Be Loyal. *It will be helpful for you to have your Bible and a copy of the commentary available as you work through this lesson.*

## Getting Started

### From the Commentary

Chapters 14—20 I have called "The Retirement of the King." During the period of time recorded by Matthew in these chapters, Jesus often withdrew from the crowds and spent time alone with His disciples. There were several reasons for these withdrawals: the growing hostility of His enemies, the need for physical rest, and the need to prepare His disciples for His future death on the cross. Unfortunately, the disciples were often caught up in the excitement generated by the crowds that wanted to make Jesus their King (see John 6:15).

—*Be Loyal,* page 117

1. Go through Matthew 14—15 and circle the times when Jesus went away to be by himself. In each case, what was the reason for His withdrawal? What do these experiences tell us about Jesus' ministry? About the challenges He faced?

*More to Consider: The Herod mentioned in 14:1 is Herod Antipas, the son of Herod the Great. His title was "tetrarch," which means "ruler over one-fourth of the kingdom." He was known as a selfish and ambitious man. Like the other Herods, he practiced the Jewish religion when it served his purposes. How is this like or unlike the way some leaders practice their faith today?*

2. Choose one verse or phrase from Matthew 14—15 that stands out to you. This could be something you're intrigued by, something that makes you uncomfortable, something that puzzles you, something that resonates with you, or just something you want to examine further. Write that here.

# Going Deeper

*From the Commentary*

> Herod Antipas was guilty of gross sin: He had eloped with
> Herodias, the wife of his half-brother Philip I, divorcing
> his own wife and sending her back to her father, the king
> of Petra (Lev. 18:16; 20:21). Herod listened to the voice of
> temptation and plunged himself into terrible sin.
>
> But there were other voices that God sent to warn Herod.
>
> The voice of the prophet (Matt. 14:3–5).
>
> The voice of conscience (Matt. 14:1–2).
>
> The voice of Jesus (Luke 23:6–11).
>
> The voice of history.
>
> —*Be Loyal*, pages 118–19

3. Review Matthew 14:1–12. Why did God send Herod so many warnings
about his sin? What does this story illustrate about the ways God speaks?
About people's willingness to listen? About what we can expect to happen
to someone who confronts sin the way John did?

## From the Commentary

> Jesus and His disciples desperately needed rest (Mark 6:31), yet the needs of the multitudes touched His heart. The word translated "moved with compassion" literally means "to have one's inner being (viscera) stirred." It is stronger than sympathy. The word is used twelve times in the Gospels and eight of these references are to Jesus Christ.
>
> —*Be Loyal*, page 120

4. Review Matthew 14:13–21. How does this passage illustrate Jesus' compassion for the people? Why is it significant that Jesus showed compassion even though He and the disciples were undoubtedly exhausted from all their work? What does this tell us about the role of compassion in a disciple's life?

## From the Commentary

> Here were more than five thousand hungry people, and the disciples had nothing to feed them! ... When they

considered the time (evening) and the place (a desolate place), they came to the conclusion that nothing could be done to solve the problem. Their counsel to the Lord was: "Send them away!"

How like many of God's people today. For some reason, it is never the right time or place for God to work. Jesus watched His frustrated disciples as they tried to solve the problem, but "He Himself knew what He was intending to do" (John 6:6 NASB). He wanted to teach them a lesson in faith and surrender.

—*Be Loyal*, page 121

5. What were the lessons the disciples learned from the feeding of the multitudes (Matt. 14:14–21)? What steps did they take to solve the problem? How are these steps applicable to problems faced by Christians today? Share an example of how this works.

## From the Commentary

John recorded the reason why Jesus was in such a hurry to dismiss the crowd and send the disciples back in the boat:

The crowd wanted to make Jesus king (John 6:14–15). The Lord knew that their motives were not spiritual and that their purposes were out of God's will. If the disciples had stayed, they would certainly have fallen in with the plans of the crowd, for as yet, the disciples did not fully understand Christ's plans.

—*Be Loyal*, page 122

6. In what ways did the storm on the sea illustrate that the disciples still didn't fully understand Jesus' plans? What important lessons did they learn in that experience? How are those lessons appropriate for us today? What does this whole section of Matthew tell us about the role of trust in the life of a disciple?

## From the Commentary

In Matthew 15, we see the Lord in conflict with His enemies (Matt. 15:1–11), teaching His own disciples (Matt. 15:12–20), and ministering to the needy multitudes (Matt. 15:21–31). This is the pattern during this period of withdrawal.

Our Lord's greatest concerns are *truth* and *love*. He taught the Jewish leaders the *truth* and exposed their hypocrisy, and He showed the Gentile crowds *love* as He met their needs. By studying these two concerns, we can understand the message of this chapter.

—*Be Loyal,* page 129

7. Go through chapter 15 and circle examples of Jesus teaching the truth and showing the Gentile crowds love. How do these two contrasting elements work together to illustrate the message of the chapter? What are the great concerns Jesus exposes in this chapter?

## From Today's World

The role tradition plays in today's society is less significant than it was in Jesus' day. In a highly mobile culture, traditions often get left behind in favor of new routines to match the new town, job, or circumstance. But those traditions that do hang around carry a lot of weight in families, workplaces, and communities. Whether supported by the expression "That's the way we've always done it" or inspired by good memories, traditions can have a great deal of influence.

8. How can you know when a tradition is a good thing or something that's missing the point? At what point does a tradition become cumbersome or get in the way of truth? How does Jesus' explanation about the "clean and unclean" in Matthew 15:1–20 shed light on the difference between the "letter of the law" and the "intent of the law"? What implications does this have for how we practice long-standing traditions?

### From the Commentary

> Not only did Jesus *teach* that no foods were unclean, but He practiced His teaching by going into Gentile territory. He left Israel and withdrew again, this time into the area of Tyre and Sidon. The Gentiles were "unclean" as far as the Jews were concerned. In fact, Jews referred to the Gentiles as "dogs." That Jesus would minister to Gentiles was no surprise (Matt. 12:17–21), though at that time, the emphasis was on ministering to Israel (Matt. 10:5–6).
>
> —*Be Loyal*, page 132

9. Even though He was focusing His ministry on Israel during this time, Jesus practiced what He was preaching by going into Gentile territory. What

does this tell us about Jesus' understanding of His own ministry? Of God's greater plan for the Gentiles? What lessons can we draw from this example?

## From the Commentary

> Jesus healed a man [in the region of the Decapolis (a predominantly Gentile territory)] who was deaf and mute (Mark 7:31–37). Even though the Lord cautioned the man to be silent, he and his friends spread the account of the miracle abroad. This apparently caused a great crowd to gather—including people who were lame, blind, mute, and crippled (maimed). Jesus healed these people, and the Gentiles "glorified the God of Israel."
>
> —*Be Loyal*, page 133

10. As you read Matthew 15:21–39, what do you notice about the contrast between the Gentiles' response to Jesus and the previously described response of the Jewish leaders? How did Jesus' miracles among the Gentiles glorify God? What spiritual lessons can we glean from this passage?

## Looking Inward

Take a moment to reflect on all that you've explored thus far in this study of Matthew 14—15. Review your notes and answers and think about how each of these things matters in your life today.

*Tips for Small Groups: To get the most out of this section, form pairs or trios and have group members take turns answering these questions. Be honest and as open as you can in this discussion, but most of all, be encouraging and supportive of others. Be sensitive to those who are going through particularly difficult times and don't press for people to speak if they're uncomfortable doing so.*

11. In Matthew 14—15, we learn that Jesus needed to take time alone for a variety of reasons. When have you felt a similar need to spend time alone with God? How do you make time for that "recharging" or "rest" in your life? What happens when you don't take time alone? Think of practical ways to "get away to the mountain" during your busy workweek.

12. Have you ever felt like the disciples when they found themselves unable to see how they might feed a large crowd? Describe those circumstances. What caused you to doubt God's provision? If you eventually did learn

to trust God, how did the situation turn out? What lessons did you learn through that experience?

13. What traditions or habits do you practice that get in the way of living out God's truth? Why is it difficult to let go of those things? What are some ways you can move toward letting go of wrong traditions in favor of those that glorify God and help move His plan forward?

## Going Forward

14. Think of one or two things that you have learned that you'd like to work on in the coming week. Remember that this is all about quality, not quantity. It's better to work on one specific area of life and do it well than to work on many and do poorly (or to be so overwhelmed that you simply don't try).

Do you need to learn to trust God's provision? Do you need to reconsider the traditions you hold too tightly? Be specific. Go back through Matthew 14—15 and put a star next to the phrase or verse that is most encouraging to you. Consider memorizing this verse.

*Real-Life Application Ideas: Hold a "feeding the five thousand" dinner at your home with family and friends. Serve a small amount of food to a large group and use that time to talk about how God provides even when we think we don't have enough. Enjoy the bread of fellowship and conversation rather than the stuffing of stomachs.*

## Seeking Help

15. Write a prayer below (or simply pray one in silence), inviting God to work on your mind and heart in those areas you've previously noted. Be honest about your desires and fears.

*Notes for Small Groups:*

- *Look for ways to put into practice the things you wrote in the Going Forward section. Talk with other group members about your ideas and commit to being accountable to one another.*

- *During the coming week, ask the Holy Spirit to continue to reveal truth to you from what you've read and studied.*

- *Before you start the next lesson, read Matthew 16—18. For more in-depth lesson preparation, read chapters 13–15 in* Be Loyal.

# Glory and Rebuke
## (MATTHEW 16—18)

*Before you begin …*
- *Pray for the Holy Spirit to reveal truth and wisdom as you go through this lesson.*
- *Read Matthew 16—18. This lesson references chapters 13–15 in* Be Loyal. *It will be helpful for you to have your Bible and a copy of the commentary available as you work through this lesson.*

## Getting Started

### From the Commentary

The events recorded in Matthew 16 form a dramatic turning point in our Lord's ministry. For the first time, He mentioned the church (Matt. 16:18) and openly spoke about His death on the cross (Matt 16:21). He began to prepare the disciples for His arrest, crucifixion, and resurrection. But, as we shall see, they were slow to learn their lessons.

The theme of *faith* runs through the events of this chapter.

—*Be Loyal,* page 139

1. Go through Matthew 16 and underline verses that illustrate the theme of faith. Why do you think this becomes an important theme in light of what's already come before in Jesus' story?

*More to Consider: Read Matthew 16:5–12 and Mark 8:14–21. Why did the disciples misunderstand Jesus here? What are other examples where Jesus spoke spiritually but the people thought He was speaking literally? (See John 3:4; 4:11; 6:51–56; and 6:63.)*

2. Choose one verse or phrase from Matthew 16—18 that stands out to you. This could be something you're intrigued by, something that makes you uncomfortable, something that puzzles you, something that resonates with you, or just something you want to examine further. Write that here.

## Going Deeper

### From the Commentary

If anyone else asked, "Whom do men say that I am?" we would think him either mad or arrogant. But in the case of Jesus, a right confession of who He is is basic to salvation

(Rom. 10:9–10; 1 John 2:18–23; 4:1–3). His person and His work go together and must never be separated. It is amazing to see how confused the public was about Jesus (John 10:19–21). Perhaps, like Herod, the people thought Jesus was John raised from the dead.

Peter had the correct response: "Thou are the Christ [the Messiah], the Son of the living God!"

It should be noted that there had been other confessions of faith prior to this one. Nathanael had confessed Christ as the Son of God (John 1:49), and the disciples had declared Him God's Son after He stilled the storm (Matt. 14:33). Peter had given a confession of faith when the crowds left Jesus after His sermon on the Bread of Life (John 6:68–69). In fact, when Andrew had brought his brother Simon to Jesus, it was on the basis of this belief (John 1:41).

—*Be Loyal*, page 142

3. How did Peter's confession differ from the ones that preceded it? (Review the Scripture passages listed in the excerpt above for context.) What is significant about Jesus' response to Peter's confession? What do you think Jesus meant about building his church on "this rock" (Matt. 16:18)?

## From the Commentary

> Having declared His person, Jesus now declared His
> work, for the two must go together. He would go to
> Jerusalem, suffer and die, and be raised from the dead.
> This was His first clear statement of His death, though
> He had hinted at this before (Matt. 12:39–40; 16:4; John
> 2:19; 3:14; 6:51). "And He was stating the matter plainly"
> (Mark 8:32 NASB).
>
> —*Be Loyal*, page 146

4. Why is it important that Jesus first declared His person, then His work?
What does Peter's response (Matt. 16:22) tell us about Peter? About the
disciples' understanding of what it meant to be the Messiah? How would
Jesus' response to Peter have been received by the disciples? What does it
tell us today about the mission of a disciple of Christ?

## From the History Books

The church that Jesus said He would build upon the "rock" has changed
dramatically over the years. In the earliest days, the "church" referred
to a body of believers and not at all to the building in which they met.

While the disciples often met to worship in homes, explosive growth in the number of Christians demanded larger and larger facilities to accommodate the crowds. This led to the use of public meeting places and, eventually, the creation of buildings meant exclusively for worship by Christians.

5. What challenges did the early church face that were unique to their time in history? What are some of the unique challenges faced by the church today? In what ways has the idea of "the church" shifted over time? What are some practical ways to make sure the church is all about people and not about a building?

*From the* **Commentary**

> Matthew and Mark state that the Transfiguration took place "after six days," while Luke says "about an eight days after" (Luke 9:28). There is no contradiction; Luke's statement is the Jewish equivalent of "about a week later." During that week, the disciples must have pondered and discussed what Jesus meant by His death and resurrection. No doubt they were also wondering what would happen to the Old Testament promises about the

kingdom. If Jesus were going to build a church, what would happen to the promised kingdom?

The Transfiguration revealed four aspects of the glory of Jesus Christ the King.

The glory of His person.

The glory of His kingdom.

The glory of His cross.

The glory of His submission.

—*Be Loyal*, pages 149–52

6. Read Matthew 17:1–13. How does the Transfiguration reveal Jesus' glory? (See the different aspects in the excerpt above.) The disciples had been taught that Elijah would come first to prepare for the establishing of the kingdom. What did the killing of the "Elijah" forerunner suggest about what would likely happen to the Messiah and those who follow Him as King?

## From the Commentary

We move from the mountain of glory to the valley of need. The sudden appearance of Jesus and the three disciples startled the multitudes (Mark 9:15). The distraught father had brought his demonized son to the nine disciples, begging them to deliver him, but they could not. The scribes had noticed their failure and were using it as a reason for argument. And while the disciples were defending themselves, and the scribes were accusing them, the demon was all but killing the helpless boy.

Our Lord's first response was one of sorrow. As He beheld the embarrassed disciples, the arguing scribes, and the needy father and son, He groaned inwardly and said, "How long shall I be with you and put up with you?" (Luke 9:41 NASB).

—*Be Loyal*, page 153

7. Why do you think Jesus responded the way He did in Matthew 17:17? What does this contrast to the previous scene (the Transfiguration) tell you about the turmoil that preceded the creation and growth of the early church?

*More to Consider: Read Matthew 17:24–27. This is the only time Scripture records Jesus performing a miracle to meet His own needs. What was Jesus' explanation for this miracle? In what ways was this not a selfish miracle?*

## From the Commentary

In Matthew 18, Jesus rebuked His disciples for their pride and desire for worldly greatness, and He taught them the three essentials for unity and harmony among God's people. The first of these is humility.

—*Be Loyal*, page 159

8. Review Matthew 18:1–14. How does this passage describe the need for humility? What is the example of humility offered here? What does the metaphor of cutting off hands and feet (18:8) tell us about the cost of humility? What does all of this say about why humility is essential for us?

*From the Commentary*

> We don't always practice humility. There are times when, deliberately or unconsciously, we offend others and hurt them. Even the Old Testament law recognized "sins of ignorance" (Num. 15:22–24), and David prayed to be delivered from "secret faults" (Ps. 19:12), meaning "faults that are even hidden from my own eyes." What should we do when another Christian has sinned against us or caused us to stumble? Our Lord gave several instructions.
>
> —*Be Loyal*, page 162

9. What are the instructions Jesus gives in Matthew 18:15–20? Why is it important to keep the matter private if possible? (See also Gal. 6:1.) Why is it sometimes necessary to air the matter honestly before the whole church?

*From the Commentary*

> When we start living in an atmosphere of humility and honesty, we must take some risks and expect some dangers. Unless humility and honesty result in forgiveness,

relationships cannot be mended and strengthened. Peter recognized the risks involved and asked Jesus how he should handle them in the future.

But Peter made some serious mistakes. To begin with, he lacked humility himself. He was sure his brother would sin against him, but not he against his brother! Peter's second mistake was in asking for limits and measures. Where there is love, there can be no limits or dimensions (Eph. 3:17–19).

—*Be Loyal*, pages 164–65

10. What do you think Peter was thinking when he said "seven times," even though the rabbis thought three times were sufficient? How might Peter have responded to Jesus' answer? How easy is it for you to continually offer forgiveness? How does our willingness or reluctance to forgive reveal the condition of our hearts?

## Looking Inward

Take a moment to reflect on all that you've explored thus far in this study of Matthew 16—18. Review your notes and answers and think about how each of these things matters in your life today.

*Tips for Small Groups: To get the most out of this section, form pairs or trios and have group members take turns answering these questions. Be honest and as open as you can in this discussion, but most of all, be encouraging and supportive of others. Be sensitive to those who are going through particularly difficult times and don't press for people to speak if they're uncomfortable doing so.*

11. Who do you say Jesus is? What are the practical implications of your answer? How does your belief about who Jesus is affect your daily decisions?

12. What does "church" mean to you? In what ways do you see yourself as a member of the long line of believers that preceded you all the way back to the disciples and the early church? How do you live out your role as a member of Christ's church?

13. Describe a time when offering forgiveness was difficult for you. What is the most challenging thing for you about offering forgiveness? What does Jesus' message to Peter tell you about how you ought to respond when wronged?

## Going Forward

14. Think of one or two things that you have learned that you'd like to work on in the coming week. Remember that this is all about quality, not quantity. It's better to work on one specific area of life and do it well than to work on many and do poorly (or to be so overwhelmed that you simply don't try).

Do you need to better understand your role in the church? Do you need to work on forgiving someone in particular or being more forgiving in general? Be specific. Go back through Matthew 16—18 and put a

star next to the phrase or verse that is most encouraging to you. Consider memorizing this verse.

> *Real-Life Application Ideas: Meet with church leaders to learn more about how your church can live out the commission of the early church. Consider the obstacles that today's church has in reaching out to people with humility and honesty. Then work together with other members to put into practice any ideas you come up with.*

## Seeking Help

15. Write a prayer below (or simply pray one in silence), inviting God to work on your mind and heart in those areas you've previously noted. Be honest about your desires and fears.

*Notes for Small Groups:*

- *Look for ways to put into practice the things you wrote in the Going Forward section. Talk with other group members about your ideas and commit to being accountable to one another.*

- *During the coming week, ask the Holy Spirit to continue to reveal truth to you from what you've read and studied.*

- *Before you start the next lesson, read Matthew 19—20. For more in-depth lesson preparation, read chapters 16–17 in* Be Loyal.

# Instructions
## (MATTHEW 19—20)

*Before you begin ...*
- *Pray for the Holy Spirit to reveal truth and wisdom as you go through this lesson.*
- *Read Matthew 19—20. This lesson references chapters 16–17 in Be Loyal. It will be helpful for you to have your Bible and a copy of the commentary available as you work through this lesson.*

## Getting Started

### From the Commentary

The King's "retirement" from the crowds was about to come to an end. But the attacks of the enemy would grow more intense, culminating in His arrest and crucifixion. The religious leaders had already tried to ensnare Him with questions about the Sabbath and signs, and they had failed. They tried again, this time with a most controversial issue—divorce.

—*Be Loyal,* page 169

1. Why do you think the leaders chose the topic of divorce to challenge Jesus at this time in His ministry? What made it a hot potato to handle?

*More to Consider: Paul used marriage as an illustration of the intimate relationship between Christ and the church (Eph. 5:22–23). In what ways does Jesus' response to the issue of divorce apply to this analogy as well?*

2. Choose one verse or phrase from Matthew 19—20 that stands out to you. This could be something you're intrigued by, something that makes you uncomfortable, something that puzzles you, something that resonates with you, or just something you want to examine further. Write that here.

# Going Deeper

## From the Commentary

> By going back to the original Edenic law, Jesus reminded
> His listeners of the true characteristics of marriage. If we
> remember these characteristics, we will better know how
> to build a happy and enduring marriage.
>
> —*Be Loyal*, page 170

3. What was Jesus' initial response to the Pharisees' question? How would
an answer referencing Scripture have been received by the religious leaders?
In what ways were the Pharisees trying to trick Jesus with their questioning?
How did Jesus answer their challenge?

## From the Commentary

> Like many people who "argue religion," these Pharisees
> were not interested in discovering truth. They were
> interested only in defending themselves and what they
> believed. This was why they asked about the Jewish law of
> divorce recorded in Deuteronomy 24:1–4.
>
> —*Be Loyal*, page 172

4. Review the Mosaic law of divorce in Deuteronomy 24:1–4. Why was this a good law? How did the Pharisees intend to trap Jesus by referencing this law? How did Jesus answer in a way that both acknowledged the law and provided new understanding?

## From Today's World

The topic of divorce is both important and controversial today. The divorce rate continues to climb (at this writing, it is nearly 50 percent, although the number is lower for first marriages at 41 percent, and higher for second and third marriages). Divorce has invaded even the homes of Christian leaders. Someone has commented that couples "are married for better or worse, but not for long." Today, all states essentially grant what is called a "no-fault divorce"—a divorce whereby the spouse doesn't have to prove that the other spouse did something wrong.

5. Clearly, the topic of divorce continues to be a contentious one, both outside and within the church. What truths from Jesus' answer to the Pharisees still apply today to this issue? How do the Mosaic laws apply (or not apply) today? What might Jesus say in answer to the rising frequency of divorce in the world today? How does this issue affect the church?

## From the Commentary

> We cannot follow the King without paying a price. After all, He went to the cross for us! Have we the right to escape sacrifice and suffering? In Matthew 19:16—20:34, our Lord explains the rightful demands that He makes on those who want to trust Him and be His disciples.
>
> Each of the first three gospels records [the "rich young ruler"] event. When we combine the facts, we learn that this man was … probably the ruler of a synagogue. We can certainly commend this young man for coming publicly to Christ and asking about external matters. He seemed to have no ulterior motive and was willing to listen and learn.
>
> —*Be Loyal*, page 179

6. What does the story of the rich young ruler tell us about the cost of discipleship? How do you think the man was hoping Jesus would answer when he asked what good thing he could do to gain eternal life? Why did the man make the wrong decision? What are some of the things today that get in the way of someone entering the kingdom of God?

*From the Commentary*

> Nowhere in the Bible are we taught that a sinner is saved
> by selling his goods and giving money away. Jesus never
> told Nicodemus to do this, or any other sinner whose
> story is recorded in the Gospels. Jesus knew that this man
> was covetous; he loved material wealth. By asking him
> to sell his goods, Jesus was forcing him to examine his
> own heart and determine his priorities. With all of his
> commendable qualities, the young man still did not truly
> love God with *all* of his heart.

> —*Be Loyal*, page 181

7. What are common causes of a divided heart (like the one the rich young
man had)? What are other examples from Scripture, or even in your own
experience, that illustrate how God uses our circumstances to move us to
examine our hearts?

## *From the Commentary*

> Peter was quick to see the contrast between the wealthy ruler
> and poor disciples. "We have forsaken all, and followed thee;
> what shall we have therefore?" Jesus gave them a marvelous
> promise of rewards in this life and in the next. They would
> even share thrones when He established His kingdom.
> Whatever good things they had forsaken for His sake would
> be returned to them a hundredfold. In other words, they
> were not making sacrifices—they were making investments.
> But not all of the dividends would be received in this life.
>
> —*Be Loyal*, page 182

8. What do you think prompted Peter's question? How does Jesus' comment
in Matthew 19:30 speak to possible misinterpretations of his previous promise
of rewards? Read the next parable in 20:1–16. How does this parable connect
with 19:30? How does it connect to Peter's concern about being properly
compensated?

## From the Commentary

> For the third time, Jesus announced His arrest, crucifixion, and resurrection (see Matt. 16:21; 17:22). In the previous announcements, He had not specified how He would die. But now He clearly mentioned the cross. He also clearly mentioned His resurrection, but the message did not penetrate the disciples' hearts.
>
> In contrast to this announcement of suffering and death, we have the request of James and John and their mother, Salome.
>
> —*Be Loyal*, page 184

9. Based on what follows in the conversation with James and John and their mother, what did they hear in Jesus' words? What did they miss? What was wrong about their request? What motivated it? How are Christians today driven by the same wrong motivations?

*From the Commentary*

> The word *minister* in Matthew 20:26 means "a servant."
> Our English word *deacon* comes from it. The word *servant*
> in Matthew 20:27 means "a slave." Not every servant was
> a slave, but every slave was a servant. It is sad to note
> in the church today that we have many celebrities, but
> very few servants. There are many who want to "exercise
> authority" (Matt. 20:25), but few who want to take the
> towel and basin and wash feet.
>
> —*Be Loyal*, pages 185–86

10. How did Jesus' teaching about servanthood answer James and John's request? In what ways does this speak to issues in today's church? How does the concept of serving others fly in the face of our culture's emphasis on success and fame?

## Looking Inward

Take a moment to reflect on all that you've explored thus far in this study of Matthew 19—20. Review your notes and answers and think about how each of these things matters in your life today.

*Tips for Small Groups: To get the most out of this section, form pairs or trios and have group members take turns answering these questions. Be honest and as open as you can in this discussion, but most of all, be encouraging and supportive of others. Be sensitive to those who are going through particularly difficult times and don't press for people to speak if they're uncomfortable doing so.*

11. How has the issue of divorce affected your life? What do you see in Jesus' teaching that speaks to the issue today? What is a Christlike response to those who have been through divorce?

12. What are some examples of the "cost of discipleship" that you have paid? In what ways is it easy for you to follow Christ? What are the costs that make it difficult? What steps can you take to let go of the things that divide your heart?

13. When have you suffered from issues of pride? When have you humbled yourself and become the servant? How does loving the "things of this world" make it difficult to serve Christ? How can you go about becoming the "least of these"?

## Going Forward

14. Think of one or two things that you have learned that you'd like to work on in the coming week. Remember that this is all about quality, not quantity. It's better to work on one specific area of life and do it well than to work on many and do poorly (or to be so overwhelmed that you simply don't try).

Do you need to work on your marriage or learn how to respond in a Christlike manner to friends who've been divorced? Do you need to work on issues of pride? Be specific. Go back through Matthew 19—20 and put a star next to the phrase or verse that is most encouraging to you. Consider memorizing this verse.

*Real-Life Application Ideas: In this section of Matthew, Jesus makes a critical point about the role of serving. Look for specific ways you can serve others in the coming week—but make sure your motives are right and you're not looking for recognition for your acts. Some ideas might include mowing a neighbor's lawn, baking cookies and leaving them with an anonymous note at a friend's house, offering to be the carpool driver on days when it's someone else's turn. These don't need to be big acts—sometimes it's the little acts of service that make the biggest difference.*

## Seeking Help

15. Write a prayer below (or simply pray one in silence), inviting God to work on your mind and heart in those areas you've previously noted. Be honest about your desires and fears.

*Notes for Small Groups:*

- *Look for ways to put into practice the things you wrote in the Going Forward section. Talk with other group members about your ideas and commit to being accountable to one another.*
- *During the coming week, ask the Holy Spirit to continue to reveal truth to you from what you've read and studied.*
- *Before you start the next lesson, read Matthew 21—23. For more in-depth lesson preparation, read chapters 18–20 in* Be Loyal.

# Judgment and Denunciation
## (MATTHEW 21—23)

*Before you begin ...*

- *Pray for the Holy Spirit to reveal truth and wisdom as you go through this lesson.*
- *Read Matthew 21—23. This lesson references chapters 18–20 in* Be Loyal. *It will be helpful for you to have your Bible and a copy of the commentary available as you work through this lesson.*

## Getting Started

### From the Commentary

Since it was Passover, there were probably about two million people in and around Jerusalem. This was the only time in His ministry that Jesus actually planned and promoted a public demonstration. Up to this time, He had cautioned people not to tell who He was, and He had deliberately avoided public scenes.

—*Be Loyal,* page 189

1. Why do you think Jesus chose the time of the Passover to promote a public demonstration? How is this situation different from the previous events when Jesus told others not to tell who He was? How does this fit in with the greater story yet to come?

*More to Consider: Read Psalm 118:25–26. The people were quoting from this passage when they shouted "Hosanna," which means "Save now!" Why would the people have chosen this particular response to Jesus' arrival?*

2. Choose one verse or phrase from Matthew 21—23 that stands out to you. This could be something you're intrigued by, something that makes you uncomfortable, something that puzzles you, something that resonates with you, or just something you want to examine further. Write that here.

# Going Deeper

*From the Commentary*

> Jesus performed two acts of judgment: He cleansed the temple, and He cursed a fig tree. Both acts were contrary to His usual manner of ministry, for He did not come to the earth to judge, but to save (John 3:17). Both of these acts revealed the hypocrisy of Israel: The temple was a den of thieves, and the nation (signified by the fig tree) was without fruit.
>
> —*Be Loyal*, page 191

3. What is the significance of Jesus' acts of judgment in Matthew 21:12–22? Why do you think these occur right after His final arrival into Jerusalem? What are the evidences of hypocrisy He was challenging? How does Jesus' response in these situations apply to the church today? What are the great hypocrisies Jesus would be compelled to challenge?

*From the Commentary*

> The series of parables in Matthew 21:23—22:14 grew out
> of the demand of the chief priests and elders for Jesus to
> explain what authority He had for cleansing the temple.
> As the custodians of the spiritual life of the nation, they
> had the right to ask this question. But we are amazed
> at their ignorance. Jesus had given them three years of
> ministry, and they still would not face the facts. They
> wanted more evidence.
>
> In taking them back to the ministry of John, Jesus was
> not trying to avoid the issue. John had prepared the way
> for Jesus. Had the rulers received John's ministry, they
> would have received Jesus. Instead, the leaders permitted
> Herod to arrest John and then to kill him. If they would
> not accept the authority of John, they would not accept
> the authority of Jesus, for both John and Jesus were sent
> by God.
>
> —*Be Loyal*, page 193

4. How do the parables in this section speak to the concerns of the chief
priests and elders? What does the manner in which Jesus introduces
these parables tell us about Jesus' understanding of the religious leaders'
concerns? What did their "I don't know" response say about them?

## From Today's World

Hypocrisy didn't disappear from the church when Jesus turned over the moneychangers' tables—it is just as prevalent in today's church as it was in the Jewish culture of Jesus' time. Today, however, the line between legitimate business and profiteering has become thin in Christian culture. Few would dispute that it is necessary to make money in order to continue a venture—even a venture that is rooted in ministry. But a quick scan of recent headlines will likely reveal news about the more questionable financial practices of some so-called ministries.

5. How do we determine what is a legitimate approach to funding church ministries and what is worthy of table turning? How does hypocrisy in these matters damage the church? What should a Christlike response be to those people or organizations that live out the hypocrisy that so angered Jesus?

## From the Commentary

In spite of the fact that the Pharisees and the Herodians had been worsted, the Sadducees entered the field and tried *their* attack. Keep in mind that this group accepted only the authority of the five Books of Moses. The Sadducees did not believe in a spirit world or in the doctrine of the resurrection (Acts 23:8). They had often challenged the Pharisees to prove the doctrine of the resurrection from Moses, but the Pharisees were not too successful with their arguments.

The Sadducees based their disbelief of the resurrection on the fact that no woman could have seven husbands in the future life.

*—Be Loyal*, page 201

6. What false assumptions did the Sadducees make in order to support their disbelief in the resurrection? What are some similar false assumptions people make today about the future life? Why do you think this challenge is immediately followed by the Pharisee's question about "the greatest commandment"? (See Matt. 22:34–40.) How would Jesus' answer have been received by those who were so quick to attack Him?

*From the Commentary*

When He was ministering on earth, Jesus often accepted the messianic title "Son of David" (see Matt. 9:27; 12:23; 15:22; 20:30–31; 21:9, 15). The rulers had heard the multitudes proclaim Him as "Son of David" when He rode into Jerusalem. The fact that He accepted this title is evidence that Jesus knew Himself to be the Messiah, the Son of God. As God, He was David's Lord, but as man, He was David's Son, for He was born into the family of David (Matt. 1:1, 20).

The scholars in that day were confused about the Messiah. They saw two pictures of the Messiah in the Old Testament and could not reconcile them. One picture showed a Suffering Servant, the other a conquering and reigning Monarch. Were there two Messiahs? How could God's servant suffer and die? (See 1 Peter 1:10–12.)

—*Be Loyal*, page 205

7. In Matthew 22:41–46, Jesus poses a curious question to the Pharisees. How is this question about Christ's relationship to David linked to the religious leaders' challenges of Jesus? Why did Jesus' question silence the leaders? What does this say about Jesus' understanding of His role in God's plan? About the Pharisees' role?

## From the Commentary

> Perhaps we should remind ourselves that not all of the Pharisees were hypocrites. There were about six thousand Pharisees in that day, with many more who were "followers" but not full members of the group. Most of the Pharisees were middle-class businessmen, and no doubt they were sincere in their quest for truth and holiness.
>
> In Matthew 23:1–12, Jesus explained the basic flaws of pharisaical religion.
>
> —*Be Loyal*, pages 207–8

8. Go through Matthew 23:1–12 and circle the flaws that Jesus describes. Why is each of these a flaw? How are these flaws still evident today in religious society? How are we to avoid these flaws?

## From the Commentary

> We must not read the series of denunciations in Matthew 23:13–36 with the idea that Jesus lost His temper and was bitterly angry. Certainly He was angry at their sins and

what those sins were doing to the people. But His attitude was one of painful sorrow that the Pharisees were blinded to God's truth and to their own sins.

—*Be Loyal*, pages 209–10

9. What is your initial reaction to this series of "woe to you" statements? How might the Pharisees have reacted to this? What was Jesus' purpose in stating each of these things? What does it mean to be a "blind guide" (Matt. 23:16)? Are these denunciations applicable to today's church? Explain.

*More to Consider: Compare and contrast the eight woes in Matthew 23:13–36 with the Beatitudes found in Matthew 5:1–12.*

## From the Commentary

Jesus spoke the words of lamentation in Matthew 23:37–39 as a sincere expression of His love for Jerusalem, and His grief over the many opportunities for salvation that they had passed by. "Jerusalem" refers to the entire nation of Israel. The nation's leaders had been guilty of repeated crimes as they rejected God's messengers, and even killed some of them. But in His grace, Jesus came to gather the people and save them.

—*Be Loyal*, page 213

10. In what ways is Jesus' lamentation a fitting close to this section of Matthew? How might the repeated challenging of Jesus' authority have played into this lamentation? What similar ache might Jesus have for the world today? What responsibility does Jesus give His people today to reach out to those who are "desolate"?

## Looking Inward

Take a moment to reflect on all that you've explored thus far in this study of Matthew 21—23. Review your notes and answers and think about how each of these things matters in your life today.

*Tips for Small Groups: To get the most out of this section, form pairs or trios and have group members take turns answering these questions. Be honest and as open as you can in this discussion, but most of all, be encouraging and supportive of others. Be sensitive to those who are going through particularly difficult times and don't press for people to speak if they're uncomfortable doing so.*

11. Has Jesus ever confronted sin in your life as He confronted it at the temple? What are some areas you continue to struggle with that need to be addressed? How might you go about addressing those areas?

12. In what ways have you struggled with hypocrisy? What are the greatest challenges in being consistent about your faith? Have you ever spoken out about someone's hypocrisy? Describe that situation. What is the proper Christlike response to these sorts of situations?

13. Review the words Jesus speaks to the Pharisees in Matthew 23:1–36. Are you guilty of any of these flaws? If so, how can you overcome them? What are the specific things you can do to avoid a pharisaical faith?

## Going Forward

14. Think of one or two things that you have learned that you'd like to work on in the coming week. Remember that this is all about quality, not quantity. It's better to work on one specific area of life and do it well than to work on many and do poorly (or to be so overwhelmed that you simply don't try).

Do you need to examine your heart for hypocrisy? Do you need to learn how to be less pharisaical? Be specific. Go back through Matthew 21—23 and put a star next to the phrase or verse that is most encouraging to you. Consider memorizing this verse.

*Real-Life Application Ideas: Invite the wise counsel of close friends to examine your habits and practices to see if you are being hypocritical with your faith. Be aware that when you invite this sort of review, the truth could be difficult to hear. Pray before you begin this process that you will be open to seeing those places in your life that need cleansing, and that you will find the will and the means to become whole and singularly purposed in your faith.*

## Seeking Help

15. Write a prayer below (or simply pray one in silence), inviting God to work on your mind and heart in those areas you've previously noted. Be honest about your desires and fears.

*Notes for Small Groups:*

- *Look for ways to put into practice the things you wrote in the Going Forward section. Talk with other group members about your ideas and commit to being accountable to one another.*

- *During the coming week, ask the Holy Spirit to continue to reveal truth to you from what you've read and studied.*

- *Before you start the next lesson, read Matthew 24—26:56. For more in-depth lesson preparation, read chapters 21–23 in* Be Loyal.

# Return
## (MATTHEW 24—26:56)

*Before you begin …*
- *Pray for the Holy Spirit to reveal truth and wisdom as you go through this lesson.*
- *Read Matthew 24—26:56. This lesson references chapters 21–23 in Be Loyal. It will be helpful for you to have your Bible and a copy of the commentary available as you work through this lesson.*

## Getting Started

### From the Commentary

The events described in Matthew 24:4–14 are "the beginning of sorrows" (Matt. 24:8). The image of a woman in travail is a picture of the tribulation period (Isa. 13:6–11; 1 Thess. 5:5). Let's consider some of the significant events that will occur at the beginning of this period:

Religious deception (vv. 4–5).

Wars (v. 6).

Famines (v. 7a).

Death (vv. 7b–8).

Martyrs (v. 9).

Worldwide chaos (vv. 10–13).

Worldwide preaching (v. 14).

—*Be Loyal,* pages 218–19

1. What does the disciples' question in Matthew 24:3 tell you about their growing concern about God's unfolding plan? How might they have reacted to Jesus' response? How does Jesus' response speak to a sense of urgency? Which of these events might have been most troubling to the disciples? Which are most troubling to today's church?

2. Choose one verse or phrase from Matthew 24—26:56 that stands out to you. This could be something you're intrigued by, something that makes you uncomfortable, something that puzzles you, something that resonates with you, or just something you want to examine further. Write that here.

# Going Deeper

*From the Commentary*

> The midpoint of the tribulation period (Matt. 24:15–22)
> is most important, for at that time an event will take
> place that was prophesied centuries ago by Daniel (Dan.
> 9:24–27). Please notice that this prophecy concerns only
> the Jews and the city of Jerusalem ("thy people and ...
> thy holy city," Dan. 9:24). To apply it to the church or to
> any other people or place is to misinterpret God's Word.
>
> —*Be Loyal*, page 219

3. Review Matthew 24:15–22. What are the specific events that occur
during this time? What instructions does Jesus give to those who are
around during this time in history (24:16–18)? How might the disciples
have responded to these dramatic words?

*From the History Books*

The end of the world has been predicted for centuries by individuals and
groups representing all kinds of religious points of view. Many ancient
cultures made predictions about the end of the world. Some of these

predictions can be explained away as the rantings of madmen, but even these typically draw followers, pulling them out of traditional Christianity or other religious practices.

4. What is the draw of "end of the world" theories or beliefs? Why are people so easily captured by such predictions? In what ways does Jesus' explanation shed light on the truth about the end of the age? In what ways does it confuse readers? Why are there multiple interpretations about what will happen in the end times? What is a Christian's responsibility when considering these differing interpretations?

*From the Commentary*

> World conditions at the end of the Tribulation will be so terrible that men will wonder if any relief will come, and this will give false christs opportunities to deceive many. Satan is capable of performing "lying wonders" (2 Thess. 2:9–12; Rev. 13:13–14). The fact that a religious leader performs miracles is no assurance that he has come from God. Many Jews will be deceived, "for the Jews require a sign" (1 Cor. 1:22). Jesus performed true signs in His Father's

name, and the nation rejected Him (John 12:37ff.). Satan's miracles they will accept.

*—Be Loyal*, pages 221–22

5. Why do you suppose God allows false christs to do miraculous signs? What does this say about God's greater plan for the world? How will people know that the christs and prophets are false? Are there examples of false prophets today? What makes them false?

*More to Consider: Matthew 24:27 indicates that the return of Jesus to the earth will be sudden, like a stroke of lightning. How does this help answer the concern about determining false prophets?*

## From the Commentary

Matthew 24:36 makes it clear that no one will know the day or the hour of the Lord's coming. But they can be aware of the movements of events and not be caught by surprise.

*—Be Loyal*, page 223

6. Review Matthew 24:32–44. What are some of the events or clues that warn of the Lord's coming? What does it mean, practically speaking, to "keep watch"? Even though this section is speaking specifically to Israel, how does it also apply to us today?

*More to Consider: Respond to the following statement: The purpose of prophecy is not to entertain the curious but to encourage the consecrated. How is this supported by what Jesus says in Matthew 24?*

## From the Commentary

We must not be surprised that our Lord suddenly changed from discussing His return as it relates to Israel to His return as it relates to the church. It is not uncommon in Scripture for a speaker to change emphasis right in the middle of a sentence.

When Jesus Christ returns and takes His church to heaven, He will sit on His judgment seat and judge His own people (Rom. 14:10–12; 2 Cor. 5:8–11). He will not judge our sins, because these have already been judged on the cross (Rom. 8:1–4). But He will judge our works and will give rewards to those who have earned them (1 Cor. 3:9–15). The parables in Matthew 24:45—25:30 suggest that Jesus will judge three different groups of professed believers.

—*Be Loyal*, pages 227–28

7. For what behaviors are people judged in Matthew 24:45—25:30? What does this passage suggest about how we ought to live out our faith? Can a person having saving faith in Christ and yet be like the man who hid what his master had entrusted to him (25:24–25)? Explain.

## From the Commentary

Matthew 25:31–46 explains to us how Jesus Christ will judge the Gentile nations. The word *nations* in Matthew 25:32 means "Gentiles," and it is in the neuter gender in the Greek. The word *them* in that same verse is in the masculine. This means that the nations will be gathered before Jesus Christ, but He will judge them as *individuals*. This will not be a judgment of groups

(Germany, Italy, Japan, etc.) but of individuals within these nations.

—*Be Loyal*, page 232

8. Can a person have saving faith in Christ and yet behave like the goats in Matthew 25:41–46? Explain. Who are the "brothers of mine" (v. 40)? What does this parable teach us about how we're to live out our faith in everyday life?

## From the Commentary

Events were now moving to a climax. The King was preparing to suffer and die. This preparation was in three stages and at three different locations. As we examine these stages, we can see the growing conflict between Christ and the enemy.

The first location was at Bethany. Matthew does not claim to give us a chronological account of the events of the last week. At this point (26:1–16), he inserted a flashback to describe the feast in Bethany and the beautiful act that Mary performed. The religious leaders were meeting to plot against Jesus, but His friends were meeting to show their love and devotion to Him.

The second location was in the upper room. It was necessary to purchase and prepare the materials needed for the Passover feast. It was also necessary to find a place in crowded Jerusalem where the feast could be held. Jesus sent Peter and John to make these important preparations (Luke 22:8).

The third location was at Gethsemane. This was a private garden at the Mount of Olives that Jesus had often used as a retreat (John 18:2).

—*Be Loyal*, pages 237–42

9. Who were the main players and what was the theme in the Bethany story (Matt. 26:1–16)? In the upper room (26:17–30)? In the garden (26:31–56)? What are the key moments in each story? How do all three of these events together move God's plan of salvation forward toward a climax?

*More to Consider: The word* Gethsemane *means "oil press." Why is this meaningful to Jesus' story?*

## From the Commentary

> We must not think that it was the fear of death that made our Lord to agonize in the garden. He did not fear death, but faced it with courage and peace. He was about to "drink the cup" that His Father had prepared for Him, and this meant bearing on His body the sins of the world (John 18:11; 1 Peter 2:24).
>
> Jesus was not wrestling with God's will or resisting God's will. He was yielding Himself to God's will. As perfect Man, He felt the awful burden of sin, and His holy soul was repelled by it. Yet as the Son of God, He knew that this was His mission in the world. The mystery of His humanity and deity is seen vividly in this scene.
>
> —*Be Loyal*, page 243

10. How does Jesus' prayer in the garden illustrate His understanding of the role God has given Him? Why is He overwhelmed with sorrow (Matt. 26:38)? Why do we need to know that Jesus experienced such intense and painful emotions, and yet remained committed to God's will?

# Looking Inward

Take a moment to reflect on all that you've explored thus far in this study of Matthew 24—26:56. Review your notes and answers and think about how each of these things matters in your life today.

*Tips for Small Groups: To get the most out of this section, form pairs or trios and have group members take turns answering these questions. Be honest and as open as you can in this discussion, but most of all, be encouraging and supportive of others. Be sensitive to those who are going through particularly difficult times and don't press for people to speak if they're uncomfortable doing so.*

11. What is most troubling or difficult to understand about Jesus' teaching on the "end of the age"? In what ways should this teaching influence the way in which you live out your faith? Is it important for you to understand the events that will unfold at the end of the age? Why or why not?

12. What are some of the things Jesus might say about your life that would put you among the sheep and not the goats? If you are not saved by works, but by faith, why are these works so important as evidence of genuine faith? What moves you to do good things for other people in need?

13. What aspects of Jesus' preparation for the cross touch you most deeply? Why are you moved by these events? What can you learn from the way Jesus moved through these trying times to help you when you are facing trials? What role does trust play in Jesus' story? In yours?

## Going Forward

14. Think of one or two things that you have learned that you'd like to work on in the coming week. Remember that this is all about quality, not quantity. It's better to work on one specific area of life and do it well than to work on many and do poorly (or to be so overwhelmed that you simply don't try).

Do you need to further explore Jesus' words on the end of the age? Do you need to take inventory of the ways in which you have served Christ? Be specific. Go back through Matthew 24—26:56 and put a star next to the phrase or verse that is most encouraging to you. Consider memorizing this verse.

> *Real-Life Application Ideas: Jesus' teaching on the end times can be difficult to follow, especially in light of the other prophetic teachings in Daniel and Revelation. Seek out a Bible study on these books of the Bible (or one on the general theme of the end times) and spend time with it to better understand the differing interpretations of these events. Then, rather than focusing on which is "better" or "right," consider how all of them inspire Christians to live their lives for Christ today.*

## Seeking Help

15. Write a prayer below (or simply pray one in silence), inviting God to work on your mind and heart in those areas you've previously noted. Be honest about your desires and fears.

*Notes for Small Groups:*

- *Look for ways to put into practice the things you wrote in the Going Forward section. Talk with other group members about your ideas and commit to being accountable to one another.*

- *During the coming week, ask the Holy Spirit to continue to reveal truth to you from what you've read and studied.*

- *Before you start the next lesson, read Matthew 26:57—28. For more in-depth lesson preparation, read chapters 24–26 in* Be Loyal.

# Trial into Victory

## (MATTHEW 26:57—28)

*Before you begin ...*

- *Pray for the Holy Spirit to reveal truth and wisdom as you go through this lesson.*
- *Read Matthew 26:57—28. This lesson references chapters 24–26 in* Be Loyal. *It will be helpful for you to have your Bible and a copy of the commentary available as you work through this lesson.*

## Getting Started

### From the Commentary

After Jesus was arrested, He was taken to the house of Annas, the former high priest who was the father-in-law of Caiaphas, the high priest (John 18:13ff). Annas, a shrewd politician, was something of a "godfather" in the temple establishment. Jesus then was taken to Caiaphas and, in the morning, to the meeting of the Sanhedrin. They turned Him over to Pilate who tried to put Him under Herod's jurisdiction (Luke 23:6–12). But Herod sent Him back to Pilate.

Matthew centered his attention on four persons who were involved in the trial and suffering of the Lord.

Caiaphas (Matt. 26:57–68)

Peter (Matt. 26:69–75)

Judas (Matt. 27:1–10)

Pilate (Matt. 27:11–26)

—*Be Loyal,* pages 247–51

1. What role does each person above play in Jesus' trial and suffering? What is unique about each of the characters? What does this diverse group teach us about how God uses people to work out His plan of salvation? What can we learn from each of these people that can be applied to our lives today?

*More to Consider: Read Psalm 22 for a vivid picture of crucifixion. The Jews could not crucify criminals (although they sometimes stoned them to death). (See Deut. 21:23.) How does God overcome this obstacle in order to fulfill the prophecy of Jesus' death on the cross? (See Matt. 27:24–26.)*

2. Choose one verse or phrase from Matthew 26:57—28 that stands out to you. This could be something you're intrigued by, something that makes you uncomfortable, something that puzzles you, something that resonates with you, or just something you want to examine further. Write that here.

## Going Deeper

*From the Commentary*

> The official indictment against Jesus was that He claimed
> to be the King of the Jews (Matt. 27:37). The soldiers took
> advantage of this accusation and paid "homage" to the
> King. It was a cruel way to treat an innocent prisoner who
> had already been scourged.
>
> —*Be Loyal*, page 255

3. Read Matthew 27:27–31. Why didn't Pilate do anything to stop the mocking? Why didn't Jesus fight against it? What might the disciples have been thinking and feeling as they witnessed this? How do Christians today deal with being mocked by those who disagree with them? Should we take it as passively as Jesus did? Explain.

*From the Commentary*

> Crucifixion was the most shameful and painful way to execute a criminal. Jesus did not simply die; He died "even the death of the cross" (Phil. 2:8). Roman citizens ordinarily were not crucified. In fact, crucifixion was never mentioned in polite society, so degrading was this form of capital punishment.
>
> —*Be Loyal*, page 256

4. Why did God choose to have His Son die on the cross and not in some other way? What can the cross teach us that other methods of death might not have?

*From the Commentary*

> Jesus was crucified at nine o'clock in the morning; and from nine until noon, He hung in the light. But at noon, a miraculous darkness covered the land. This was not a sandstorm or an eclipse, as some liberal writers have suggested. It was a heaven-sent darkness that lasted for three

hours. There were three days of darkness in Egypt before Passover (Ex. 10:21–23), and there were three hours of darkness before the Lamb of God died for the sins of the world.

—*Be Loyal*, page 258

5. What is the significance of the three hours of darkness that fell upon the land during Jesus' crucifixion? In what ways is this similar to the three days of darkness in Egypt? (See Ex. 10:21–23.) What does the darkness symbolize?

## From the Commentary

Were it not for the intervention of Joseph of Arimathea and Nicodemus (John 19:38), the body of Jesus might not have had a decent burial. Joseph and Nicodemus had come to believe in Jesus, even though they had not openly testified of their faith. God kept them hidden, as it were, that they might care for the body of Jesus. Since Joseph was a rich man, and he prepared the new tomb, he helped in the fulfillment of prophecy, Isaiah 53:9—"He

was assigned a grave with the wicked, and with the rich
in his death" (NIV).

—*Be Loyal*, page 260

6. Review Matthew 27:57–66. Compare the responses of those who loved
Jesus to those of the Jewish leaders. Do you think the Pharisees' reason for
placing guards around the tomb was purely because they feared the body
might be stolen? Why or why not? How was this decision by the Jewish
leaders important to God's plan for Jesus' death and resurrection?

## From the Commentary

The women who had lingered at the cross came early to the
tomb, bringing spices that they might anoint Jesus' body.
They thought He was dead. In fact, they wondered how
they would move the huge stone that blocked the entrance
to the tomb (Mark 16:3). It is remarkable that they did not
believe in His resurrection when He had taught this truth
repeatedly (Matt. 16:21; 17:23; 20:19; 26:32).

—*Be Loyal*, page 263

7. Why do you think the women (and others) had a hard time believing in the resurrection? How might Jesus' death have affected their belief in Jesus' other teachings? Why is the resurrection so critical to Christian faith? What does it prove about Scripture? What does it say about our own future? In what ways does it give us power?

## From Today's World

In a world defined by technology that can do nearly anything we ask of it, there is little room for wonder or surprise. It's not long ago that people were wowed by special effects in movies and children could be mesmerized by the simplest sleight of hand proffered by a parent. (The old quarter-behind-the-ear trick was nearly always a winner.) But today, even the youngest children have a hard time being impressed by things that once seemed almost magical. The idea of a tombstone being rolled away by angels might be explained away as a "special effect" by this current generation of technologically savvy children and adults.

8. How can we as a Christian culture understand and pass along the great power that was revealed with Jesus' resurrection? What are the challenges in teaching today's young people about the Easter miracle? (See Matt. 28:2.)

## From the Commentary

> The remarkable change in the early believers is another
> proof of Jesus' resurrection. One day they were dis-
> couraged and hiding in defeat. The next day they were
> declaring His resurrection and walking in joyful victory.
> In fact, they were willing to die for the truth of the resur-
> rection. If all of this were a manufactured tale, it could
> never have changed their lives or enabled them to lay
> down their lives as martyrs.
>
> —*Be Loyal*, page 265

9. What evidence do we have in Matthew 28 that helps support the truth of
Jesus' resurrection? (See also 1 Cor. 15:3–8.) Why is it important to know
that people saw the risen Christ? How important is this to the existence
and growth of the early church? What would have happened to the church
had Jesus not risen from the dead and made Himself known?

*More to Consider: Review Matthew 28:11–15. In what ways does this
action help to prove the validity of Jesus' resurrection?*

*From the Commentary*

> Matthew 28:18–20 is usually called "the Great Commission,"
> though this statement is no greater than that in any of the
> other gospels, nor is it the last statement Jesus made before
> He returned to heaven. However, this declaration does apply
> to us as believers.
>
> *—Be Loyal*, page 268

10. What "authority" does Matthew 28:18 refer to? What are the activities
that the disciples were commissioned to do? What does Jesus promise
in 28:20 for those who take upon themselves this commission? Is the
commission the same today as it was in Jesus' time? Explain.

## Looking Inward

Take a moment to reflect on all that you've explored thus far in this study
of Matthew 26:57—28. Review your notes and answers and think about
how each of these things matters in your life today.

*Tips for Small Groups: To get the most out of this section, form pairs or trios and have group members take turns answering these questions. Be honest and as open as you can in this discussion, but most of all, be encouraging and supportive of others. Be sensitive to those who are going through particularly difficult times and don't press for people to speak if they're uncomfortable doing so.*

11. Consider Caiaphas, Peter, Judas, and Pilate. In what ways do you relate to one or more of these important figures in Christian history? What are some of the lessons you can learn and apply from their stories?

12. What is your emotional reaction to the description of Jesus' crucifixion? How does Jesus' death and resurrection affect the way you live your daily life? What are you most thankful for about Jesus' sacrifice? How do you (or will you) bring glory to God for all that He has done through His Son?

13. In what ways are you living out the Great Commission? When have you experienced resurrection power in your life? What are some practical steps you can take to spread the good news to others?

## Going Forward

14. Think of one or two things that you have learned that you'd like to work on in the coming week. Remember that this is all about quality, not quantity. It's better to work on one specific area of life and do it well than to work on many and do poorly (or to be so overwhelmed that you simply don't try).

Do you need to ask forgiveness for disbelief or denying Christ? Do you need to explore how you might help make disciples and train them to obey all that Jesus commanded? Be specific. Go back through Matthew 26:57—28 and put a star next to the phrase or verse that is most encouraging to you. Consider memorizing this verse.

*Real-Life Application Ideas: No matter what the date is on your calendar, plan and carry out a special Easter celebration. This could be anything from a simple dinner with friends to a full-blown program for your church. Be sure to involve family members of all ages. Use this time to underscore the truth that Jesus' death and resurrection is something to be thankful for every day of the year, not just around Easter.*

## Seeking Help

15. Write a prayer below (or simply pray one in silence), inviting God to work on your mind and heart in those areas you've previously noted. Be honest about your desires and fears.

*Notes for Small Groups:*
- *Look for ways to put into practice the things you wrote in the Going Forward section. Talk with other group members about your ideas and commit to being accountable to one another.*
- *During the coming week, ask the Holy Spirit to continue to reveal truth to you from what you've read and studied.*

# Summary and Review

*Notes for Small Groups: This session is a summary and review of this book. Because of that, it is shorter than the previous lessons. If you are using this in a small-group setting, consider combining this lesson with a time of fellowship or a shared meal.*

> *Before you begin...*
> - *Pray for the Holy Spirit to reveal truth and wisdom as you go through this lesson.*
> - *Briefly review the notes you made in the previous sessions. You will refer back to previous sections throughout this bonus lesson.*

## Looking Back

1. Over the past ten lessons, you've examined Matthew's gospel. What expectations did you bring to this study? In what ways were those expectations met?

2. What is the most significant personal discovery you've made from this study?

3. What surprised you most about Matthew's telling of the gospel story? What, if anything, troubled you?

## Progress Report

4. Take a few moments to review the Going Forward sections of the previous lessons. How would you rate your progress for each of the things you chose to work on? What adjustments, if any, do you need to make to continue on the path toward spiritual maturity?

5. In what ways have you grown closer to Christ during this study? Take a moment to celebrate those things. Then think of areas where you feel you still need to grow and note those here. Make plans to revisit this study in a few weeks to review your growing faith.

## Things to Pray About

6. Matthew's gospel is rich with history and packed with Jesus' teaching. As you reflect on the words Matthew has written, ask God to reveal to you those truths you most need to hear. Revisit the book often and seek the Holy Spirit's guidance to gain a better understanding of what it means to be righteous before God.

7. The content of Matthew covers the entire story of Jesus' birth, life, death, and resurrection. It includes many of Jesus' parables as well as key teaching moments such as that found in the Sermon on the Mount (Matthew 5—7). Take time to think about the aspects of Jesus' life that have touched you most. Pray about each of these things.

8. Whether you've been studying this in a small group or on your own, there are many other Christians working through the very same issues you discovered when examining Matthew's gospel. Take time to pray for each of them, that God would reveal truth, that the Holy Spirit would guide you, and that each person might grow in spiritual maturity according to God's will.

## A Blessing of Encouragement

Studying the Bible is one of the best ways to learn how to be more like Christ. Thanks for taking this step. In closing, let this blessing precede you and follow you into the next week while you continue to marinate in God's Word:

*May God light your path to greater understanding as you review the truths found in the gospel of Matthew and consider how they can help you grow closer to Christ.*